VGM Opportunities Series

OPPORTUNITIES IN
FASHION CAREERS

Roslyn Dolber

Foreword by
Diane Von Furstenburg
Designer

VGM Career Horizons
a division of *NTC Publishing Group*
Lincolnwood, Illinois USA

Cover Photo Credits:

Front cover: All photos courtesy of
Fashion Institute of Technology.

Back cover: upper left and upper
right, Fashion Institute of Technology;
lower left, The School of the Art Institute
of Chicago.

Library of Congress Cataloging-in-Publication Data

Dolber, Roslyn.
  Opportunities in fashion careers / Roslyn Dolber.

      p.   cm. — (VGM opportunities series)
    ISBN 0-8442-4022-2 (hardbound) — ISBN 0-8442-4023-0
(softbound)
    1. Fashion—Vocational guidance.   I. Title. II. Series.
TT507.D58   1992
687'.023'73—dc20   92-16079
                                                          CIP

ABOUT THE AUTHOR

Roslyn Dolber has been an enthusiastic proponent of the fashion industry for over twenty years and is presently the Director of Placement at the Fashion Institute of Technology (FIT) in New York City. Thoroughly familiar with the wide range of opportunities in the fashion field, she has counseled and placed thousands of students in positions throughout the industry. Her professional affiliations include the New York State Guidance and Counseling Association and the Metropolitan New York College Placement Officer's Association.

In addition to her duties at FIT, Mrs. Dolber finds time to speak extensively on fashion-related careers in the New York metropolitan area and has contributed articles on this subject to several industry publications. She has completed a filmstrip for high school and college students about preparing for and surviving the job interview and also has authored *Opportunities in Retail Careers*. She serves as a representative for the fashion industry as an expert witness in legal and court-related cases.

FOREWORD

I found fashion almost by accident. In 1969 I was 22 years old and visiting the U.S. from Europe to do some modeling. Fashion here was either wild hippy garb, stiff little designer dresses or drip-dry polyester, and I thought there was something missing . . . chic, affordable dresses that real women of all ages and sizes could wear from a day at the office to a night out.

Following my instincts, I went to Italy to do some "homework" and worked for an Italian textile mill that developed wonderful knit jersey fabrics. I learned all about knitting, printing and garment manufacturing and proceeded to design the simple little wrap dress I had imagined. I broke all the rules, combining a sporty t-shirt fabric with a feminine body-conscious style, because I really believed that it was the right product at the right time. Luckily, so did Diana Vreeland, the powerful editor of American *Vogue,* and with her advice that I rent a hotel room to show my dresses to buyers during market week, I was on my way!

The most important thing in pursuing a career in fashion is to believe in yourself and your vision. Nothing can compete with passion. When a company making my women's line went out of business, just as I was getting a great reaction to a new dress concept I was testing, I quickly took the business in-house so as not to lose the momentum. Being able to sense and quickly react to changes in the marketplace is critical to surviving in today's constantly changing times. You have to be flexible and creative enough to come up with plan B when plan A fails, and then have the "guts" to put it into action!

Contrary to popular belief, this business is 99 percent hard work and 1 percent glamour. You have to be willing to do whatever it takes to get the job done. For most of us, there is no time clock and no pay for overtime. When my first dress shipment was held up by U.S. Customs because all of the labels were mistakenly printed in Italian, I was at the airport until midnight rewriting them in English, so I could honor my first shipping deadlines.

In this age of specialization, a focused product and clearly defined market niche are probably even more important than when I first started out. Your vision must make sense for the times and fill a specific need for your target customer or it will get lost in a sea of others. You must be able to at least understand both the nuts-and-bolts of daily operations (sourcing, production, selling-in to the stores, shipping, distribution, selling-thru to the customer) as well as the romancing of the product via good public relations and publicity. And whether you're looking for a new boss/mentor to teach you the ropes, or later on a crackerjack assistant to help you get your job done, always surround yourself with the best people you can find. You can tell a lot about people by the team they play on.

The biggest challenge in fashion for me is staying one step ahead of the times, the trends and the customer. The biggest reward is meeting customers wherever I go, listening and talking to them, and seeing them respond to my products. *Bonne chance* (as we say in French) or "good luck" in all your endeavors . . . the future is yours for the taking!

Diane Von Furstenberg

INTRODUCTION

The world of fashion—it's exciting, fast moving, and alive with change, and it may hold the beginnings of a challenging and rewarding career that's just right for you.

Though fashion has long been a basic concern of many men and women, it was not until the Industrial Revolution that the fashion industry provided a livelihood for thousands and thousands of people. But even the impact that fashion had on the lives of people immediately after the Industrial Revolution cannot compare to the influence it exerts on our lives today. For as modern technology has increased our leisure time, so, too, it has increased the role fashion plays in our daily lives. Today, with great advances in apparel technology and training, it seems that the variety of articles manufactured by the fashion industry is virtually limitless. Likewise, the variety of career opportunities available to the creative, industrious, and enthusiastic individual is greater than ever.

Countless interests and skills are applied in the field of fashion, which in its versatility produces such different items as clothing and accessories for children, men, and women; textiles; cosmetics; plastics; and home furnishings. The manufacturing, buying, selling, marketing, packaging, and displaying of these goods are all important parts of the industry.

Because of the vast size of the fashion industry and its related fields, four major areas will be described to present a picture of some of the many opportunities available. They are apparel design, apparel production, textiles, and fashion merchandising.

You are fortunate to have the opportunity to choose among the fascinating careers available to you within the fashion world. Begin to think about and learn about the areas that may be right for you. Now, more than ever, young men and women have the opportunity to explore every aspect of the work and make sound decisions about their exciting futures.

It is estimated that in your lifetime you will work approximately forty years. It is your duty to yourself to ensure that those years are exciting and satisfying. Don't assume that a work situation always has to be routine and dull. It can be a source of continued learning and pleasure from the day you begin your first job.

There is every reason for you to choose a career that is right for you. With enough information about various career paths and an understanding of your own interests and abilities, you can set your goals and aim for them. Begin to think of matching your skills and aptitudes with a career. Then you can prepare for entry-level jobs in the area that seems most satisfying to you. Remember, the choice is yours!

CONTENTS

clerk or head of stock. Assistant buyer. The buyer or department head. The merchandise manager. Fashion coordinator. Assistant to the fashion coordinator. The store manager. Assistant store manager. Resident buying offices and central buying offices. Thinking of your own business?

CHAPTER 1

APPAREL DESIGN

Fashion is often described as the current style that is followed by a large number of people at any one time. In this way fashion often reflects the tastes and values of the times. Fashion is as old as time. It concerns not only what we wear, but the style or way in which we use clothing and related items to shield our bodies from the elements and adorn ourselves colorfully and imaginatively. Students of history are just as interested in the fashions of a given society as are students of fashion design. Fashion has become a part of every aspect of our lives, from the design of our clothing to our color-coordinated kitchens. We are all part of a fashion-oriented world.

The fashion industry is vast and complex and incorporates many parts of smaller, related industries. It deals not only with the making of clothing and accessories, but also with the fabrics, leather goods, furs, plastics, or other new synthetic materials used to make these finished products. As a result, within the fashion industry you'll find firms that develop and manufacture the fibers and yarns as well as the buttons and zippers that eventually become part of the clothing we wear or the accessories we buy. Of course the stores that sell apparel and accessories make up an essential part of the fashion world too, as do the mail-order houses from which a large portion of our country shops. The publications we read to learn the latest fashion news—newspapers, magazines, and trade journals—form yet another industry affiliated with the world of fashion. Considering all these various areas of the fashion business, it's not difficult to imagine the great wealth of career opportunities available to you.

The fashion industry deals with the design, production, marketing, and distribution of clothing and accessories for children, men, and women, and for areas of the home. This multibillion-dollar industry offers a dazzling array of products in every price range. It employs hundreds of thousands of workers and needs the talents of creative, fashion-minded men and women who have the necessary training. Entry positions and career opportunities are varied. There is room in the industry for workers with many levels of skills, interests, and educational training. Job requirements are varied enough to offer employment for the most gifted workers as well as for those who are happiest at more routine tasks. It is possible to enter some phases of the apparel industry with high school preparation and without further specialized training. However, more creative and challenging positions and those that may offer the potential for career advancement are all highly competitive. These positions tend to require a minimum of two years of specialized training at the college level, and in some areas four-year degrees are important. As in many other industries, the prospects of advancement in fashion depend upon the level of one's general and specialized education in addition to skills and personality.

Regardless of where you live, the apparel industry is important. It exists in just about every part of the country. Apparel production plants are located in every state, and of course clothing and accessories retailers are found in each major city, in every suburb, and in the smallest towns.

The apparel industry is one of the leading industries in the city and state of New York, and it is one of the most important industries in our country. Its influence is felt around the world, even on Wall Street. Some large clothing manufacturing firms have "gone public" and are listed on the stock market. Some firms are large enough to manufacture different items under several different labels. Companies whose design and sales headquarters are in New York City may oversee production of their goods as far away as Hong Kong or South America. However, the bulk of the industry is not made up of giant corporations. Rather, it is comprised of many thousands of smaller-sized firms, often family owned, that try their hand at surviving in the competitive and fast-moving garment business. It has been noted that in a typical year over a thousand of New York City's eight thousand garment manufacturing firms go out of business. They are quickly replaced with another group of ambitious men and women eager to try their luck.

Today's owners of apparel manufacturing firms are more aware of fashion than ever before. They also are more aware that they need to be knowledgeable businesspeople, because fashion is a business of high risks. But it also is a business that provides excitement and employment for over one million workers. Apparel design is creative, competitive, challenging, and oftentimes glamorous. How did it all begin?

A BRIEF HISTORY

A few hundred years ago, men as well as women in the English court were bedecked in elegant and elaborate dress. Skilled dressmakers were highly regarded and kept very busy. Wealthy customers were used to paying dearly for extravagant and fanciful clothing. Then, with the Industrial Revolution, the invention of amazing textile machines, and most importantly, the power loom, the apparel manufacturing business was born!

In America, the colonists were too busy with the more pressing business of taming a continent to be interested in such extravagance. Nonetheless, they did need to be clothed, and thus the most modest homes usually had a "clothing factory"—a loom or a spinning wheel. The whole family was likely to get involved in making garments for each member. And so in this humble fashion, the real beginnings of our garment industry were established.

After the invention of the cotton gin in 1793, small mills began weaving yards of fabric that were sold to housewives. Seamstresses were kept busy copying the latest European fashions for their wealthy American customers. A short time later, in the early 1800s, clothing itself was manufactured.

For pioneering Americans, clothing was needed above all for workers. It was all handsewn by local women. It was generally poorly made and not very fashionable. In fact, this early apparel would seem primitive compared with today's sophisticated styles.

At this time, most American women were sewing their own clothing. If they were lucky enough to afford it, they hired a seamstress to make garments from fabrics bought in a dry goods store. By 1863, Mr. Butterick offered the first paper patterns for sale and launched the home sewing industry. Then the sewing machine was invented. Think of what a wonderful development this must have been for our ancestors! A fast-growing middle class was eager to buy ready-made dresses, and the garment industry was on its way to becoming a full-fledged business.

At the beginning of this century, the finer clothing Americans wore was still styled from original designs created in Paris. But our own apparel industry was growing. Factories were getting larger in size, and immigrant labor was hired to work in the plants of New York and New England. Eventually, New York City's Lower East Side became the hub of apparel manufacturing activity.

It did not take long for New York's styles to become the standard for the rest of the country. Buyers from large out-of-town clothing stores came to New York City to see the newest designs and to place their orders for the latest fashions for each season. People began reading about fashion. Fashion magazines were becoming part of the American scene, advising men and women on current styles in clothing. Newspapers carried fashion advertising. But the best publicity came from members of high society. Fashionable dances and balls were showcases in which designers could display their most elegant creations. And anyone interested in the fashion world knew what gown was worn by which society leader. More women began to read the fashion magazines that started to promote clothing of American design. In addition to original garments created by American designers, *knockoffs,* or copies of someone else's original designs, started to be produced on a large scale. In fact, many large fashion-minded stores began to advertise "line-for-line" copies of both Parisian and American designs. This is still a part of today's garment industry.

By this time, there were several good-sized apparel manufacturing firms in the country, and they employed thousands of workers. As the American garment industry grew larger, some designers traveled to Paris to view and copy the latest fashions. With a great supply of newly arrived immigrants looking for work, apparel manufacturers had an inexpensive labor source to help them produce clothing for the American public. Large quantities of clothing were produced by manufacturers at prices lower than the cost of custom-made garments. It was also fairly common for people to buy clothing from a catalog. The manufacture of ready-made clothes greatly helped the mail-order houses that began to develop.

Dressmakers continued to go into the homes of the wealthy to measure the entire family for the new clothing they had been commissioned to make. Soon many dressmakers were able to open their own small shops. Customers could go directly to the shops to see a variety of the latest styles and be fitted for the clothing. However, large numbers of American women continued to sew clothing for themselves and their families.

When, as a result of World War II, Paris was no longer available as a source of inspiration, American designers had to rely more on their own creativity. A particular style of fashion developed that was truly American in its look, with special emphasis on sportswear. Our designers are still noted for that splendid contribution to the world of fashion. In fact, sportswear and casualwear have been the fastest growing part of the women's segment of today's garment industry. Although European designers still hold great influence on the apparel industry, American designers have gained international reputations for their achievements.

Today, New York City thrives as a very important apparel center. Other major apparel centers are in Los Angeles, Dallas, Chicago, and Atlanta. Smaller centers have developed in other areas of the country as well. The apparel industry remains the employer of more than 200,000 workers in New York City and New York state. In New York City, most apparel manufacturers occupy showrooms along Broadway and Seventh Avenue between 34th and 41st streets. In other cities there are large apparel marts where most manufacturers are concentrated.

Many people have shared in the growth of our nation's apparel industry: the engineers who developed machines and systems to mass produce huge quantities of garments, the technicians who researched the fibers and fabrics we all enjoy wearing, the investors who supplied the money and the facilities, the thousands of workers who cut and sewed and pressed and shipped the millions of garments sold, and all the imaginative promoters of fashion, including the fashion writers, photographers, models, artists, illustrators, and display workers who make fashion availabe to us. These and scores of other men and women have made the apparel industry what it is today.

You too may want to become a part of this fascinating and fast-moving world of apparel. Your choice of a career in the apparel industry should be based on your performance as a worker and your ability to work well with other people. The apparel industry seeks men and women with specialized skills to meet its growing needs. Most manufacturers work closely with well-known and accredited fashion schools and hire their graduates. Be prepared for a good deal of excitement and challenge, along with the many pressures of fast-paced activity. The apparel industry is a very hard-working one. Stamina and the ability to work quickly, often under pressure, are necessary. Good grooming and a personal fashion sense are equally important. Few jobs offer a typical nine-to-five workday, particularly when production schedules or other deadlines must be met. Overtime and irregular hours are typical in many areas of this industry.

Those employed in the apparel industry tend to change jobs frequently. This reflects the changeability and seasonal nature of much of the industry. But with less occupational security than that offered by many other businesses, what accounts for the thousands of people who seek employment in this field? Many workers will say it is the excitement and thrill of being part of a dynamic and fast-moving world. With new and interesting ideas and good skills, hard-working employees can move ahead and gain recognition.

Imagine the delight of seeing someone wear a garment you had a hand in designing! Think of the satisfaction in knowing you were part of a team of employees that launched a new look or trend that really caught on! Enthusiasm and stamina seem to be the keys here. Most employees are aware of the pitfalls and risks of this seasonal and ever-changing business. And yet, for some people, those are the very reasons that they are willing to take up the challenge and enter the competition with the drive and the determination to succeed. The lives of top-notch fashion designers are filled with hard work, glamour, and excitement. But there are really few such highly successful men and women in the field. Most employees are satisfied with the fun and excitement of being part of a lively industry that may provide recognition of their talents, a chance to express some of their creative thinking, and an opportunity to be part of the fashion scene.

IT ALL BEGAN A YEAR AGO

Let's imagine that you've just purchased a new winter coat. It's just what you hoped you would see on the rack when you went shopping. The style of the garment and its particular shade of red seem most fashionable and appealing to you. But how did the manufacturer of that garment know you would be ready to buy a bright red coat for this coming winter season?

It probably all began a year or so before the coat was even shipped to your local clothing store. A fabric stylist, whose job it is to take charge of the fabric company's colors and patterns for each season, began to research the latest textile trends. Based on years of experience and excellent fashion sense, the stylist selected a group of colors that would be presented to the firm's customers—the coat manufacturers. Of course, a swatch of bright red fabric was among the stylist's choices. Several seasons had passed since red was last fashionable, So it seemed likely that the public might be interested in buying this color again. When fashion designers start to think about the fabrics they may want to use in their new lines, they are shown the newest color choices—in this case, red.

The designer and textile stylist may discuss other possible color choices, or the designer may select and order a variety of shades of red fabric along with other colors. With an idea of the available fabrics in mind, the designer starts to create a group of forty to seventy-five sketches for the future season. Many of these design sketches are inspired by the exciting and colorful fabrics presented to the designer. A good many of the sketches will be discarded because they are too expensive to produce. Others will not be used because the owner of the firm just doesn't think they will sell. After much discussion and decision making and with the help of a skilled group of workers—assistant designers, patternmakers, samplehands, and other members of the design room team—a line, or collection, of coats is agreed on. This is the result of months of consulting, fitting, and revising.

Next, a skilled samplehand carefully sews a sample coat for each design sketch that is to be part of the line. These samples are shown to merchants who may want to buy the coats for their department stores, small shops, or mail-order customers. In addition to being good looking and stylish, the coats must be well constructed and sturdy. They also must be kept within the price range that the designer originally had in mind so that the finished product is affordable to its intended market.

During this time, the stylist at the fabric company has promoted the new group of red fabrics to many other designers in the industry. These designers also will use red for their garments as part of their winter collections.

Next, fashion reporters and fashion editors are invited to the showings of each designer's new line. They may be favorably impressed and decide to feature the new red look in their newspapers or magazines. Illustrators may sketch some of the new coat styles at the collection openings. Fashion photographers may be invited to take pictures. But buyers and merchandisers are the most important guests at each showing. If they feel the coats on display are what their customers want, they will place their orders before they leave the showroom. As orders are taken, the coats are scheduled for production so that stores will have deliveries in two or three months. Very precise instructions are rushed to the coat manufacturing plant, which is usually many miles from the design room and the showroom. Coats are cut, sewn, finished, inspected, and packed for delivery to the stores that ordered them all across the country.

Fashion writers, by this time, have already started informing the public that the newest and most exciting clothes for the coming winter season will be designed in bold shades of red. And in anticipation of the new season, cosmetic and accessory companies have begun to produce a line of items that will complement the new look.

Department stores and other large retail operations have meetings with salespeople and those involved in the merchandising and advertising areas of the business. They inform their staffs of the new look and arrange for newspaper and magazine ads. The red coat may even be selected to be part of a window display promoting the bold red look for winter.

You, as the fashion-minded customer, have already been alerted to this latest trend, and you want to be a part of it. When you walk into your local store and spot that coat, it seems just right. But it took a year's labor and the talents and skills of many workers for you to have your coat. Can you imagine yourself becoming part of this picture? If so, where do you fit? Where will your talents, abilities, and personal strengths be put to use?

APPAREL DESIGNER

Apparel or fashion designers create ideas for new styles of clothing and accessories. They may specialize in the area of children's, men's, or women's items, or in more specific areas such as coats, dresses and swimwear, or hats, shoes, and handbags. They decide what length skirt or what cut of pants we will be buying in the future and which colors will be in style.

The greatest number of apparel designers are hired by manufacturers who mass produce clothing in the lower price ranges. Designers in these volume houses seldom originate fashion; instead they tend to adapt fashionable styles to meet the price range of their customers. The medium-sized manufacturer often sells clothing in a moderate price range. One or more designers may be employed, each having an assistant or a group of design room helpers. Haute couture houses, on the other hand, cater to a very high-priced market. The number of these firms is limited, and the opportunities to enter them are for only the most gifted.

The competition is extremely high for positions in which designers have the luxury of creating garments with very few restrictions. It is a glamorous world, but the chances of succeeding in it are considerably less than those of the designer who is eager to succeed in the medium-priced or volume end of the industry. Here it is a real challenge for a skilled designer to create fashionable garments at a low or moderate price. Of course, the size of design room staffs will vary from firm to firm. A typical workroom situation would probably include a head designer, who works closely with an assistant designer, and one or two samplehands or samplemakers. Many design jobs are full-time assignments, but it also is possible for experienced designers to work on a freelance basis, or for a lucky few to be self-employed in their own businesses.

The designer is a talented artist with a strong sense of color and shape. The designer must be knowledgeable about fabrics and trimmings and be familiar with the patternmaking, fitting, draping, sewing, costing, and production process for each garment. In this way, the designer can supervise the many details that go into the completion of each garment.

Ideas are researched in art galleries, museums, libraries, and fashion centers in this country and abroad. Many designers get their inspiration from seeing swatches of fabrics, and they use textile houses as an important resource. Designers also need to be aware of world events that may strongly influence clothing trends. Music, movies, or museum shows may be a source of inspiration to a designer.

Many rough sketches are drawn to show the details of a new style. They are worked on until a series of drawings, or a collection, is completed. These final designs are then approved by the manufacturer or owner of the company. Once approved, a paper pattern is made of the sketch. Or the sketched design may take its earliest form in a material called muslin, which is draped on a dressmaker's form to the specific style the designer had in mind. Once it is cut and sewn, the garment is checked carefully by the designer for any alterations or changes in design that must be made. It is now ready to be made in a fabric version to be shown to the manufacturer. Often merchandisers or salespeople will have a chance to view and comment on the designer's samples. If the sample garment is approved, it will become part of the manufacturer's line and then be shown to buyers.

The apparel designer's duties and style of work may vary greatly. In some firms, designers may only design and supervise the workroom staff. In other cases, they may be involved in every aspect of production, from creating the original design to supervising the final alterations on the finished garment. Some designers prefer not to work out their ideas with paper and pencil in sketch form. They may experiment by draping muslin or fabric on a dressmaker's form, or they may use both methods in creating their garments.

Designers are generally expected to create four lines or collections of clothing each year. There is usually one new line for each season and some firms produce a special line for the holidays. There may be as many as 40–75 new items in each line.

Designers must also supervise and plan the work for their assistants, select fabrics and trims, help with the pricing of the garments they design, work with marketing and production workers, and attend meetings to present ideas and styles to salespeople and clients. They must work long hours to be fully aware of current and future trends. Workdays are often busy and hectic, particularly when a collection is being completed for a showing. In some small firms, designers may work without the help of an assistant designer. In medium and larger-sized firms, one or more assistant designers may aid the designer at each step of the design process.

To master all of this, fashion designers need to be imaginative and have an unusual flair for clothing and fabrics. In addition, a two-year or four-year fashion design program gives men and women the special-ized knowledge of the industry that they need. These programs gener-ally include courses in drawing, patternmaking, draping, sewing, fabrics and trimmings, principles of color and design, and the production and pricing of garments.

Designers need to be able to work comfortably with many other persons. They deal with buyers, salespeople, their own design room staff, and with management, production, and publicity teams. In this industry, it is essential to work well with others and be easy to get along with. Flexibility and cooperation are extremely important, particularly in a crowded and busy design room. But flexibility and congeniality are not to be confused with indecisiveness, for designers must be able to think on their feet and believe firmly in their own creativity, since they often must sell themselves as well as their design ideas.

ASSISTANT DESIGNER

Recent graduates of two- or four-year specialized fashion design programs often enter the apparel industry as assistant designers. An assistant learns a great deal on the job but must also be very productive, as he or she may be working right alongside the designer, helping at every stage. Generally, an assistant is responsible for following through on the designer's ideas by draping in muslin from the design sketch or by creating a paper pattern. The next step is to supervise the production of the sample garment by working closely with or supervising the samplemakers. Assistant designers may be asked to do their own sewing of the sample garment if there are no samplemakers in the workroom. Clerical duties often involve keeping records of fabric and trim purchases as well as style numbers and details of each garment that is produced. There also are appointments to be made, telephones to be answered, correspondence to be faxed or telexed overseas, and loads of pins to be picked up from the floor.

Assistants soon may find themselves helping the designer select fabric and trimmings or visiting retail stores and attending fashion shows to keep abreast of new fashion trends. After the assistant is thoroughly familiar with design room procedures, he or she may begin to consult with the designer about new designs and offer some original ideas.

When applying for the position of assistant designer, it is important to have a portfolio of ideas that displays your sense of design, color, and fabric to present to the potential employer.

SKETCHING ASSISTANT

Every designer needs to have an accurately sketched record of the items that were put into production each season. Beginners who do not wish to handle the more technical skills needed in a design room and who can draw precise sketches of finished garments may enter the industry as sketching assistants.

The fabric and trimmings used in each garment are attached or *swatched* to the sketch. Details on the construction of each item are noted on a specification sheet that is filled out by the sketching assistant. The job may involve other related clerical duties as well. It does not allow for much creativity, but can satisfy the artist who enjoys drawing precise and accurate sketches. When applying for this position, it is important to have a portfolio of detailed sketches to show to the employer.

SKETCHER

These positions are very competitive, few in number, and require outstanding illustration skills and an extremely high level of fashion sense. Expensive couture houses may require the talents of an outstanding artist who can draw freehand sketches of the designer's ideas. There also may be the opportunity for the sketcher to start offering original design ideas at some point. Sketchers can be asked to meet customers, assist with presentations of new collections, and deal with buyers. Long and irregular hours are often a part of this job. The reward is the pleasure of a behind-the-scenes look at a prestige design house and the satisfaction of having a role in its operation. When applying for this position, a portfolio of artwork must be presented to the employer. Candidates must look fashionable and be extremely well groomed and poised.

SKETCHER/STYLIST

Small new companies with limited budgets often are unable to hire a full design staff. A sketcher/stylist can be valuable by providing the owners of the firm with information about design trends and new ideas for their line. A good deal of the sketcher/stylist's time is spent in retail stores evaluating the markets and visiting fabric resources. This employee may be hired to do the more technical work that is needed, but must be available to work closely with a patternmaker or sewing contractor. The sketcher/stylist chooses fabrics and trimmings, coordinates the line, makes presentations to buyers in the showroom, and often gets involved in the promotion of the line as well. When applying for this position, a portfolio of design ideas with coordinated fabrics must be shown to the employer.

Consider the wide range of specializations that exists in the apparel industry. In the women's wear area alone, there are firms that design bridal wear, evening and cocktail wear, dresses, lingerie, loungewear, leather and suede clothing, millinery, coats, sportswear, handbags, swimwear, furs, sweater knits, maternity clothes, suits, shoes, gloves, rainwear, active sportswear, and uniforms. Firms specializing in home accessories, children's wear, and men's wear also offer a host of other possibilities.

"BE SUCCESSFUL AT SOMETHING!"

Here's how Leo, a talented and motivated designer, is moving ahead with his career in the apparel industry.

Growing up in a New York suburb, Leo remembers the emphasis placed on planning for a career, not merely earning a living. The message was, "Be successful at something!" His parents, a doctor and a lawyer, were really eager to have him follow in their professions. But Leo was simply not interested. He found himself spending most of his free time in his school's art room, painting and experimenting with color.

Although he recalls learning about many of the more traditional creative careers during his school years, he never received any information about careers in the fashion industry. While in high school, he made many trips into New York City to visit museums and art galleries, shops and boutiques. He wanted to familiarize himself with all the exciting facets of the big city. He even enrolled in an advertising design course while still in his senior year, just to explore that field of work.

Leo had heard about the Fashion Institute of Technology in New York City. He liked the idea that he could get specialized technical training combined with liberal arts courses at FIT. The well-rounded program appealed to him and also satisfied his parents, who wanted their son to earn a college degree. He put together some of his best samples of artwork for his interview at the college. He had continued to paint throughout his school years and had a fine collection of watercolor sketches to present as an indication of his artistic ability. He was open to considering either an advertising design or fashion design program, and decided to choose fashion design.

Leo worked hard to complete the comprehensive two-year program. With help from the college's placement department, he was hired as an assistant designer for a manufacturer of children's clothing. He recalls telling the employer during the interview that he was very willing and eager to do everything, and that he was certainly open to learning as much as possible on the new job. Leo is convinced that his willingness to work plus his comprehensive training helped get him his first job. He was hired and worked there for two years.

The firm was a small one, and Leo was able to work very closely with the designer and learn many aspects of the business. He was always ready to try something just a little bit different or to learn a new procedure or technique. After those two satisfying years as an assistant designer, Leo wanted to follow up on his earlier interest in the advertising field. He took the bold step of opening his own advertising business. He handled fashion accounts, record albums, and book jackets and ran his business for five years. But the apparel industry still appealed to him, particularly when he ran into his friends from his college days who were happy with their design jobs. He knew he was ready to re-enter the fashion industry and try again.

Leo had kept in touch with many of his contacts from his days as an assistant designer, and he had a good sense of the current state of the industry. He also was realistic about what he could offer an employer. With his experience in the children's wear field, he decided to aim for a design job in that area of the industry. He worked on putting together an attractive portfolio and landed a design position with a major manufacturer of children's wear. He built up a fine work record with that firm and after three years, moved to a design job in the boy's wear field.

Having gained a reputation as a skilled designer, he moved on to another boy's wear firm, where his exciting line of clothing was shown at a trade show for the boy's and men's wear industry. It was at this show that a manufacturer of men's wear noticed Leo's work and convinced him to consider a job designing men's knit shirts.

Leo decided that it was important for him to broaden his experience, and he accepted the job offer. He likes the idea that he is now a skilled men's wear designer as well as a designer of boy's wear. He still believes in going further. He dreams of designing for the women's wear market someday—better dresses or sportswear or perhaps evening wear.

He has just begun a part-time job teaching boy's wear design. Leo enjoys sharing his own knowledge and work experience with his students and wants to assist them with their career choices. He's also accepting free-lance design assignments. That's a real challenge for him, as it keeps him very busy and the pressures are great. However, Leo realizes that he can handle a very responsible full-time job, along with teaching and his free-lance work, because he is well-organized and disciplined. His school preparation and years of exposure in the industry have given him the necessary skills and techniques. He's realistic enough to know that the industry has its drawbacks as well as its appeal, and that it requires hard work, long hours, lots of dedication, and strong belief in your abilities. But Leo is still eager to have many different experiences in the various phases of the industry. His drive and talent virtually ensure his success. Of course, it's impossible to know where the future will take Leo, but he's convinced he has a great deal to offer the fashion world, and that there is a great deal in it for him.

CHAPTER 2

APPAREL PRODUCTION

More than 22,000 firms across the country today are engaged in making fabric into clothing. Of course not all of the companies perform the same function within the industry. Some companies do everything necessary from designing the garment to shipping it to a retail store in your home town. Other firms design the clothing and cut the material, but then they send the cut pieces to a sewing shop to be sewn and finished. The firm then distributes the clothing when it is completed. The people who run the sewing shops that do only sewing and finishing work are called "contractors." Contractors may get work from several different companies, or they may rely on just one company to keep them busy. This part of the apparel industry is referred to as the production field.

Apparel production is a labor-intensive industry, meaning that it takes many workers to keep it operating. Other industries may require fewer workers because they rely on automated machinery to perform many jobs. The apparel production field is large, and apparel plants or factories are located in all parts of the country. New York, Pennsylvania, California, New Jersey, Massachusetts, Illinois, and Texas are states that have great numbers of apparel plants employing thousands of workers. Ohio, Tennessee, North Carolina, Missouri, Maryland, Michigan, Florida, and Georgia also are states where many apparel factories exist.

As our population grows and the demand for clothing and accessories increases in the years ahead, men and women with training and experience in the area of apparel production can look forward to well-paying and challenging careers in this little-known field. Luckily, apparel production plants are located in small towns and large cities in every single state of the United States, including the District of Columbia. This means there are many job opportunities available in a wide variety of locations for every level of ability and interest.

The production part of the apparel industry is often overlooked by job hunters and career planners. Many students are quite familiar with the better-known design and merchandising careers, but few are aware of the opportunities available in the production field, where talent, imagination, and management potential are highly sought after and very well rewarded.

HOW IT STARTS AND WHERE IT ENDS

Let's trace the various steps that are undertaken by assorted professionals to create a finished article of clothing. Pay special attention to the many different kinds of work performed on a single item after it leaves the designer's workroom.

Suppose a *designer* has just created an exciting new style of blouse. The management of the blouse company has approved the sample and wants it in the new line for the coming season. The stage is set—now the production staff begins to play their important role. To start with, a *production patternmaker* works closely with the designer to make a perfect "master pattern" of the blouse on pieces of hard paper or fiberboard. The patternmaker translates onto paper the designer's sketch of the blouse. Each piece of the blouse is represented by a piece of the pattern. The patternmaker does this by laying out all the needed parts of the blouse on material and skillfully fitting all the pieces together. Laying the pattern out incorrectly may mean using extra material. This wasted material will cost the manufacturer money and may increase the price that the customer is charged when the blouse is purchased.

The manufacturer relies on the good judgment of the production patternmaker to keep fabric yardage down and to be as efficient and precise as possible. Patternmakers must be able to visualize from the design sketch or muslin sample the shape, size, and number of pattern pieces needed for the blouse. They also must have knowledge of fabric, body proportion, and garment construction. Most assistant patternmakers pick up the many techniques of the trade beyond their specialized training by working closely with experienced patternmakers.

Pattern graders take the hard paper pattern and copy it in a whole range of sizes so that the blouse will fit each customer properly. A grader may be given a size seven pattern for a junior blouse; from this the grader makes the same pattern in sizes five through fifteen just by carefully enlarging and reducing the master pattern. This calls for accurate and exacting work, as each piece of the pattern must be drawn neatly and precisely for the production process. Some very large plants now use computers to shorten the time needed to draw patterns for each size. More firms will move into computer-aided patternmaking in the near future as the cost of this high-tech equipment goes down. Patternmakers and their assistants often do the grading of the patterns they work on.

Training in drafting is very helpful in pattern grading, as much of the work requires using drafting tools and techniques. Computer-assisted drafting skills are important today, especially in jobs with the larger firms. There are several specialized schools that will prepare you for patternmaking and pattern grading opportunities. For entry-level positions as a patternmaker, cutting assistant, grader trainee, or marker trainee, it is advisable to complete a patternmaking technology program. Such a program will offer courses in draping, patternmaking, pattern grading, pricing of garments, production processes, textile science, and other related areas. Graduates of such a program qualify for entry positions as assistant patternmakers and graders. Later, they can move on to supervisory levels, production work, or possibly assistant design jobs. All such jobs call for neat and precise work, often performed at a fast pace and under the pressure of production schedules.

After the graded patterns are made, *spreaders* lay out the fabric the designer has chosen for the blouse on a very long table. The fabric must be smooth and straight, layer after layer without wrinkles. A machine can help the spreader get the fabric ready. *Markers* have the job of positioning the hard paper patterns on top of the layers of fabric. Then *cutters* carefully cut through the layers of fabric, several inches thick, cutting around each piece of the pattern with electric cutting machines, knives, or shears. The hundreds of pieces of cut cloth are gathered and put into bundles by *assorters* or *assemblers*. Every piece of lining, trim, or fabric needed to complete the blouse is bundled and brought to the sewing room. Here, several *sewing machine operators,* or in larger plants several hundred operators, actually sew the pieces of the blouses together.

Commercial sewing machines are more powerful and sew faster than the familiar machines used at home. Generally, each sewing machine operator will have only one specific sewing job to do on the blouse. The operator acts as a specialist in one small task needed for each garment. On the blouse we are following, certain operators will sew the seams only, others will sew on the sleeves, still others attach the collar, while the rest of the operators may work on the pockets or buttonholes or any other remaining tasks. In manufacturing a very expensive garment, it is possible for each sewing machine operator to sew the entire item of clothing. *Supervisors* direct the sewing machine operators and other workers on the factory "floor" or workroom.

The sewn blouse is now ready to be given to a *finisher* who hand sews anything that may be required to finish the garment. *Cleaners* or *trimmers* remove loose threads, lint, and spots from the finished blouse. The *presser* is next in line, neatly smoothing and shaping the blouse with a steam-pressing machine. Once folded and packed, the blouse is ready for distribution to shops across the nation.

Think of the excitement of planning and coordinating the "life" of any garment or fabric! All of this behind-the-scenes activity is planned and supervised by men and women with long work experience and/or a college background in apparel production, manufacturing management, or engineering technology. Jobs are easier to find and advancement is quicker for those with this specialized training. The technical courses required for these positions may include industrial organization, production management, apparel production, business management, labor costs, marketing, statistical analysis, labor relations, computers for business or software management, plant engineering, and accounting. In addition, good communication and problem-solving skills are essential. These workers must deal with a great many people and are responsible for clearly and accurately communicating detailed instructions, as well as working successfully with varied personalities. Good math skills are valuable for all apparel production workers. Maturity and a good sense of organization should enable experienced workers to compete for supervisory positions.

Relocation may be very much a part of the employment requirements for beginners and more advanced workers as well. Trainees who are hired by very large manufacturing firms with many production plants may be expected to move to several different factory operations. Many plants, although modern and highly sophisticated, may be located in small towns all across the nation. Opportunities for high-paying careers are much greater if apparel production workers are free to consider employment anywhere in the country.

JUNIOR ENGINEER

The piece rate for the completion of each sewing and production task is set based on reports called "time and motion" studies, which the junior engineer works out. The junior engineer works at the apparel manufacturing plant and handles engineering projects and production systems and also is involved in the physical layout of the plant. This may mean selecting machinery and choosing operations methods for optimum performance. Production forecasting and planning, as well as monitoring the overall efficiency of the plant, are also part of this job. Recommendations are then reported to the management to make needed improvements. Of course, each junior engineer works very closely with a senior engineer, who is very experienced in all production phases. In a multiplant operation, a chief engineer has total responsibility for what happens in each of the factories.

COSTING CLERK

A costing clerk is trained to set the price of sample and production garments. Piece rates also are determined, under the supervision of a costing engineer. With experience in this area, promotion is possible to the position of costing engineer. In very large operations, the supervisor of the costing department has total responsibility for all costs relating to the production of the garment.

COSTING ENGINEER

The costing engineer determines the price of producing an item of apparel or a fashion accessory. The cost of the material used, piece rates, and all other production fees are taken into consideration in determining the overall cost. This position may involve occasional travel to various plants to review the production operations and procedures, or to work with the plant manager to set piece rates for the sewing machine operators. The costing engineer may be assisted by a costing clerk and spends some time training that clerk and other clerical assistants.

PRODUCTION ASSISTANT

All production-related detail work and recordkeeping for the plant manager is handled by the production assistant. This may include keeping track of fabric and trim samples, making out the cutting tickets that give the factory important information, assisting with the production schedule in the factory, checking on the flow of work and on shipments and deliveries, and keeping sales, cutting tickets, and shipping records. The production assistant also may be responsible for quality control and for supervising cutters and production patternmakers, as well as for keeping customers informed on the progress of their orders via telephone or fax machine.

Lots of detail and figure work is involved in being the link between the design room and the factory, and between the customer and the manufacturer, but it is an excellent position if you want to get an overview of the entire manufacturing process. Production assistants may work at the design and sales headquarters rather than at the factory, but there must be constant contact with the plant manager. Good math and organizational skills, the ability to handle many details and follow up on them, and the ability to communicate well with many people are important for all these beginning positions, Demanding production schedules require workers to be accurate, thorough, and capable of working under pressure.

With experience, production assistants may move up to assistant production manager, and then to production manager. It is possible for production assistants to be promoted to piece goods buyers or merchandisers, if some flair is shown in these areas.

PRODUCTION MANAGER

The production manager is responsible for estimating all production costs, scheduling the flow of work in the plant, hiring and training new workers, overseeing the quality control of the product, and supervising all aspects of production activities in the factory. The production manager must really have a hand on the pulse of the entire operation; it is a complex task. The cutting, sewing, pressing, shipping, and warehousing functions are all part of the manager's responsibility.

QUALITY CONTROL ENGINEER

This worker develops specifications for garments and fabrics and is responsible for seeing that those standards are met in all of the manufacturing phases, including fibers, textiles, colors, and garment construction. This may involve travel to many different plant locations to check sewing operations and production procedures to try to identify and correct problems. Beginners start as assistants and gain experience by working closely with the more expert engineers. Beginners may inspect garments as they come off the production line, or as they arrive from overseas if the firm is importing merchandise. Knowledge of garment construction, new machinery and textile technology is important. The position requires workers who are detail oriented, thorough, and well organized.

THE ENGINEER WHO FLUNKED MATH

Diana was convinced she wanted to be a nurse and never dreamed she'd become an engineer!

Diana was very unhappy when her parents made it clear that they didn't want her to have a nursing career. They discouraged her from attending college and urged her to become a wife and mother. And so she did. Married at age twenty, she was the mother of two children when she was divorced seven years later.

Without any skills, she found herself relying on welfare for support for almost five years. A close friend advised her to map out a career and return to school to build her own future. Out of high school for twelve years, Diana never imagined she could do it. Her high school record was poor, and she had failed every single math course she took. She recalls that her motivation for entering college and working toward a career goal was her need to support herself and her two children. Her welfare support allowed her to enroll in a two-year program. After examining the FIT catalog carefully, Diana chose a major in apparel production: Merchandise Management. With lots of financial aid arranged through the college and a great deal of support from the faculty, Diana began the program.

Her first semester was difficult. She had forgotten the study skills and note-taking techniques that she used in high school, and she was frightened that she just wouldn't make it. With special tutoring in math, her weakest area, and lots of encouragement from her family and friends, college life began to feel more comfortable. She still had the chore of juggling a double schedule—a student during the day and the mother of two children in the evening—but Diana stayed with it. By her second year in the program, she was more at ease and found time to become active in college life. She was elected president of the Apparel Production Management Club, and by the time she was graduated from FIT, she was the winner of two awards for her outstanding achievements: a student of the year award and a one thousand dollar cash prize.

Eager to begin working, she was placed in her first assignment through the college's placement office. She left New York City for a one-month trial job in the South. It was a difficult assignment, made even tougher because she missed her children very much. She worked long hours as an assistant plant manager and soon realized the work situation was just not right for her. She decided to return home after the month's trial was over and try again. She landed a junior engineering job with a manufacturer of dolls, and spent some time doing time and motion studies—a very typical beginning assignment.

A contact in the industry alerted Diana that a manufacturer of ladies' sportswear was interested in setting up an interview with Diana. Two weeks later she met an executive of the same firm, who was very impressed with her. It was then necessary for Diana to meet another executive, who was able to conduct an interview only by arranging to meet Diana at an airport while waiting for a business flight to depart. The executive believed she would be an excellent choice for the position of costing engineer, which was open in the company. However, there were some concerns about the required two-week training period that would take Diana away from her children again. Diana assured the executive that she could handle the training period away from her family, and she was hired at the airport!

On her first trip to the main office, she managed to get caught in a blizzard and spent the night in an airport. Once the weather cleared and she arrived, she was able to deal with the training period without any difficulty. She learned all about the firm's policies and procedures and is still in touch with the home office when problems arise.

As a costing engineer, Diana had her first experience in pricing their holiday line, one of the five lines that the company manufactures each year. The company's total output represents about five hundred garments each year.

Diana sits in on costing meetings attended by all the vice-presidents of the company, as well as by the president. Such meetings are held for each line that is manufactured. Every garment in the line—about one hundred each season—is broken down into each of the operations performed by the sewing machine operators. Would you guess that a lady's blazer requires fifty-five different operations? Using a set of formulas, Diana breaks down the garment into all of the needed operations and then computes the amount it will cost her company to manufacture it. All these figures are then neatly entered on specification sheets, referred to as "spec sheets" in the industry.

Diana loves her job and all that she has learned about the costing side of the business. She thoroughly enjoys her involvement in the production area, although she is sure she would not like to have her own business in the future. Instead she'd like to work her way up in the company, earn more money, and travel to various plants around the country. And *her* young daughter does not dream of becoming a nurse. She wants to be an engineer, "just like mommy."

CHAPTER 3

THE TEXTILE INDUSTRY

Only two hundred years ago most of the fabric that our pioneering ancestors used was imported from England. In fact, the textile industry was so vital to England's economy that neither the machinery used in the production of fabric nor the people who operated the machines were allowed to leave the country. At the end of the eighteenth century, an English textile mechanic named Samuel Slater settled in Rhode Island and opened a spinning mill. With improvements in spinning and weaving techniques, Eli Whitney's invention of the cotton gin, the perfection of the knitting machine, and the development of the Jacquard loom, the textile revolution in the United States was on its way. This was the important beginning of an industry that can produce enough fabric to wrap around the Earth 250 times. What's more, our textile industry provides jobs for hundreds of thousands of men and women!

About half of all the workers in the textile industry have jobs in mills that weave fabric used in clothing or household furnishings. About one third of the workers produce the knit fabrics that we see in stockings, underwear, and other knit garments. Still other workers put color and design on the cloth or are involved in the manufacture of carpets, rugs, lace, embroideries, threads, and various sewing accessories. The production of textiles is complex and offers many varied activities and occupations, ranging from the production of yarns to the production of woven or knitted cloth and the finishing of that cloth by workers who add color, texture, pattern, and ease-of-care features.

Large textile plants are concentrated in New England—where the textile industry was born—and throughout the southeastern part of the United States, with heavy concentration in North Carolina, South Carolina, and Georgia.

In the early 1900s, the number of textile-producing plants in the Southeast grew, since that part of the country had lower labor costs, cheaper steam and electric power, and was closer to the all-important cotton crop. Today, the Northeast employs a great many workers in the manufacturing of lace, ribbon, fabric tape, and in the weaving and finishing of wool. New York City, however, remains the heart of the textile industry in terms of the designing, styling, and selling of the fabric, though some smaller design and sales centers are located in New England, Philadelphia, and on the West Coast.

As the textile industry serves one of our three basic needs—that of clothing—it is an essential part of the nation's economy, even though it is very sensitive to economic changes. It is one of the few industries in the country that places great emphasis on creativity and artistic expression.

Textile designers, colorists, stylists, merchandisers, and other skilled workers all play an important role in the creation of the more than ten thousand different designs produced every year. Imagine the range of career opportunities available for those with creative talents and the proper educational background!

Although the textile industry is one of the oldest in our country, textile advances in the last twenty years have been astonishing. Fabrics that require no ironing or that have the ability to stretch as you move were unheard of only a short time ago. The range of new fabrics includes the heat-resistant textiles used in an astronaut's space suit and even the tires on a jumbo jet. In research laboratories, more and more exciting advances are being developed for the world's increasing needs, which means that researchers are needed to produce new wonders—new finishes, new colors and dyes, new blends, and new fibers.

Merchandisers, salespeople, designers, technologists, and stylists also are needed as these areas of the industry become more sophisticated and customers want something new and different each season. There is a place in the textile industry for the scientist, the salesperson, the artist, the accountant, the production analyst, and a host of other skilled people. The textile field offers challenging and promising careers along each step of the process from fiber to finished fabric.

TEXTILE SALES

Not too many years ago, the salesperson was viewed very negatively—as a slick character without much sense of responsibility toward the customer. It was assumed that a sale was made by pressuring the client with a fast-paced sales talk. Fortunately, the image of both textile and apparel salespeople has changed greatly in the recent past.

With the wonderful technological advances of the 1950s and the 1960s, efficient new high-speed machinery became part of the textile industry. It became possible for every manufacturer to produce fabrics and garments at standard levels of quality. This brought about a new focus on salesmanship. In the early 1960s, management established an interest in training better salespeople who could help the company meet the growing competition in the years ahead. The accent was on anticipating a customer's needs and on offering a full range of services.

Today's salesperson is an important representative of the company who is able to talk intelligently and knowledgeably about a product and give reputable advice and direction to the customer. Some salespeople sell fibers to yarn manufacturers, while others may sell yarn to fabric manufacturers. Still others sell finished fabrics to garment manufacturers or makers of home furnishings. All salespeople must be fully familiar with their lines, and with their firm's policies and procedures. The salesperson also must be part technician to fully understand the basics of the textile or apparel manufacturing process, as well as being aware of fashion and color trends.

Selling the product is the most competitive area in the textile and clothing manufacturing process. It is considered a highly respectable and profitable profession for men and women who have what is sometimes called a "sales personality." Not everyone is cut out for a sales career. But for those who have the potential for sales, the opportunity and the financial gains are great.

Sales Trainee

Many large textile firms, fiber or yarn companies, or apparel manufacturers hire beginners as sales trainees. This gives recent graduates the opportunity to work closely with more experienced salespeople and allows them to have a good look at all parts of the sales department. The training period can be as brief as three months or as long as a year and a half. During this training time, the sales trainee learns as much as possible about the firm's product and production process, merchandising techniques, and about the customer's needs. All the while, valuable experience is gained for the future.

The trainee is expected to perform any duty that is related to the sales operation. Often this is as simple as hanging up samples of fabric and tidying up the showroom. More often it means becoming completely familiar with the firm's product or line; greeting customers in the sales showroom and presenting the line to them; learning to determine a customer's needs; going out with an experienced salesperson on sales calls to manufacturers or retailers; carrying the samples for the salesperson; doing all the clerical work related to each day's sales; and assisting with the billing, shipping, and handling of the orders.

Some firms have very formal training programs. Workdays are very carefully planned for the trainee, who may be asked to spend a few weeks with each senior salesperson and then spend more time in the billing or shipping departments. Other firms are more casual in the training they offer. Here, sales trainees are expected to observe the entire sales operation and pick up information with each new experience, either formally or informally. After several months of looking, listening, and learning, trainees become valued additions to any sales department.

Beginning sales trainees generally work in the company's showroom, supervised by an "inside" salesperson. Customers with appointments and some who just drop by unexpectedly will want to be shown the latest lines. The sales trainee assists the customers and the other salespeople in any way possible.

Once trainees have mastered basic sales techniques and have acquired a great deal of information about the firm's line, they may be considered for "outside" sales. This means calling on customers in their offices and bringing a line of samples along for them to view. They also may be expected to build up their group of customers and add new accounts to the firm. For people who like the idea of being on the go, rather than remaining in the sales showroom day after day, this job can be very rewarding. For those who are eager to travel out of state and feel ready to move wherever the company needs sales help, it is an excellent job to consider. Most major firms employ experienced outside salespeople who are responsible for servicing a particular part of the country, or *territory*. Thus, it is necessary to have experience as a sales trainee or showroom salesperson before being considered for an outside sales job or road sales.

Many selling positions pay a flat salary, and many pay a salary plus a percentage of the amount sold. This percentage is called a *commission*. Very experienced salespeople can expect to earn a great deal on commission. They may even have an arrangement to work on a commission basis with no salary if their sales record is very strong. However, it is recommended that beginning salespeople never work on a straight commission basis. It takes years of solid experience to build up good sales techniques and a strong customer following that can be relied upon to provide a steady income.

The Responsibility of the Salesperson

New technology and a changing marketplace make new demands on today's sales force. Successful salespeople have always had to convince, persuade, and then sell the product or service. Today's salespeople must be knowledgeable enough to educate their customers as well. Buyers may not be informed about the latest features and up-to-the-minute technology that is quickly spilling over into many facets of our lives.

An informed salesperson can fill the role of educator by explaining the uses and benefits of a new fabric or fiber and thus help secure the sale.

The successful salesperson meets complex challenges: giving attention to both the needs of the customer and the interests of the company. In addition to working hard to get as many orders as possible, it is the responsibility of the salesperson to observe what is happening in the marketplace and accurately report back to the company. This vital information can affect the production, the design, or the marketing of the company's product. As salespeople are always dealing with customers and listening to their requests and ideas, they are often the best equipped people to report back on what is current and new, and what is expected by the customer. All accounts must be visited and serviced, and follow-through on each and every order is essential. There is a need to make sure that all delivery and production commitments are kept and that the merchandise is delivered exactly as ordered. Customers must be told of changes in prices, new styles and trends, and new fabric developments. And, of course, customer complaints are always a part of the salesperson's life and must be dealt with courteously.

Although making appointments and trying to develop leads on new accounts occupy a good percentage of salespeople's time, they also must spend much time planning their sales presentations as new items are added to the line and older goods are taken out. If they are knowledgeable and familiar with the line as well as with the color, style, and fabric trends for the coming seasons, they will be able to represent their company in a professional manner, while at the same time providing their clients with the best service.

A whole new area of inside selling is growing with *telemarketing,* or selling by telephone. Important developments in communications have led many businesses to telemarketing. Many firms are able to cut costs and increase sales by allowing their road sales force to sell by phone as telemarketers. Firms no longer have to support a large outside sales staff, and thay can more easily reach new customers quickly and more successfully via the telephone.

The Sales Personality

What makes a successful salesperson? Let's examine some of the traits that comprise the "sales personality." These are often the qualities sales managers look for when they hire beginners as sales trainees.

Maturity. Can you work well under pressure? Can you deal with the strain of the selling process? Can you handle many different people who have varied personalities? Are you able to accept the rejection of your line and quickly bounce back, without feeling you are a failure if the sale is not made? A poised and self-confident candidate is definitely ahead of the game.

Aggressiveness. Can you approach a customer—perhaps even a brand-new customer—with interest and enthusiasm about your line? Can you convincingly present your firm's product and encourage the customer to buy it? Can you make sales without pushing merchandise on customers that may not really be needed? Can you give your company as much business as it can handle? Will you give up easily when you meet an uninterested buyer, or will you try to keep the contact friendly and attempt to make the sale?

Integrity. The salesperson's character and reputation in the industry may quickly determine her or his success. It is important to gain the trust and respect of customers. Having integrity means being truthful. It means dealing honestly with the customer about the product, the date of delivery, the price, and any other factors concerning the sale. Salespeople will be judged on their performance, and it is essential that they live up to all commitments that they make. Promises can be easily made to get a sale. The difficulty arises in fulfilling those promises—late shipments, undelivered merchandise, and backed-up orders soon become the mark of the unprofessional and unsuccessful salesperson.

Creativity. Do you enjoy dealing with old situations in new ways? Are you able to ask yourself, "How can I do this better?" Can you take a good look at any routine and try to improve it? Salespeople are the all-important link between the customer and the product, and by adding a bit of personal style and creativity, they can please the client as well as the firm.

Sensitivity. Will you be able to adjust to the moods of the many people you will be contacting on a daily basis? Will you be able to respect another person's point of view and still maintain your own? The ability to be sensitive to the needs and desires of the customer allows the successful salesperson to know exactly when to forge ahead and when to deal gently and tactfully with a client. In come cases, it may even mean knowing it is necessary to put off the sale and return at a more appropriate time.

Appearance. Are you interested in the latest style and do you reflect it? In the fashion world personal appearance is obviously of the utmost importance. But beware. Being flashy and overdressed can be as damaging to you as being out-of-date and out-of-style. Many textile firms tend to be fairly conservative, so a well-tailored and a well-groomed look is generally the most appropriate one.

These qualities, coupled with a strong interest in sales and the ability to communicate clearly and easily, can often be the start of a successful and financially rewarding career in textile or apparel sales. In addition, a pleasant manner, willingness to work hard, enjoying contact with people, and an assertive style are a plus. More than ever, college graduates are being sought for positions in the sales field. Major companies prefer men and women with a four-year college background, but also will consider those with a solid two-year textile background for these competitive sales trainee positions. In very small firms it may be possible to be considered for a sales trainee position without such specialized school training. Previous sales experience, even on a part-time or summer basis, is often deemed sufficient.

Think seriously about a career in sales. Today's salesperson is well regarded as a leader in business and as a professional in the fashion field.

TEXTILE DESIGN

Are you fascinated by beautiful patterns or fabrics and textile products? If you have a fine sense of color, some degree of manual dexterity, and an interest in the fashion field, you should consider a career in textile design.

Long before any fabric is produced, the design must be created. Men and women who have two to four years of specialized education beyond high school in textile design find challenging careers creating patterns or designs that are woven, knitted, or printed on fabrics. Most designers work in New York City, where the designing and styling departments of the major textile firms are generally located. With school training in drawing, use of color, and specific textile design techniques, artists begin to design original patterns. Generally, print designers paint their designs on paper for eventual reproduction by printing machines. This procedure differs somewhat for the designers of woven fabrics, who may work out their ideas in another way. Designers of woven fabrics may work directly on small hand looms, weaving their sample fabrics. Knit designers may create their samples on a hand-knitting machine. Many designers now use a computer to assist in the design process.

All designers must have a good knowledge of textiles, fabric construction, and production processes in addition to a strong feeling for pattern and color. Designers of woven or knitted cloth have less need for a fine drawing ability but require more knowledge of yarns, technical processes, and machine capabilities.

Designers may be given a particular direction or "fashion look" by the textile stylist, or they may be familiar enough with trends and styles to know what fashion looks consumers will be eager to buy in the future. Working a year or more ahead of the current season, textile artists create original designs that are then sold to the manufacturers of the clothing we buy. Some artists design only the fabrics used in the home furnishings industry. Their designs are then used in the manufacture of draperies, slipcovers, pillows, and upholstered items. Other fabric is designed to be sold to people who sew at home—this is called over-the-counter fabric. Whatever the final use of the fabric, the textile field may provide you with an exciting career once you have the required specialized training.

Textile Colorist

Graduates of college textile design programs usually enter this creative end of the textile industry as textile colorists. This position allows a beginner to gain speed and a sense of color by learning to match and paint various color combinations or arrangements on a design created by the textile artist or designer. You may have seen a particular textile design that was available in three or four different combinations of color. It is the textile colorist's responsibility to decide which combinations of color will appeal most to the customer and skillfully apply those colors to the design with paints or dyes.

The well-trained colorist is an important member of the designer's team and must quickly learn how colored dyes will look on almost any type of fabric swatches. They often research files of older textiles to get color information.

The textile colorist generally does not paint directly on fabric. Initially, the print designs and colorings are on paper. Most of the creative designing and coloring process is all worked out on paper, allowing for many changes before final approval is given for the production of each design. Then specific instructions are sent to the mill where the next stage of the fabric manufacturing process begins.

Colorists and textile designers must be very neat and careful workers who can follow precise instructions and work at a fast pace. There are many deadlines that must be met to keep the expensive production of the fabric on schedule. A two- or four-year college program in textile design qualifies you for a position as an entry-level textile colorist. Courses may include the study of woven and printed fabrics, color fundamentals, nature studies, and creative principles. A portfolio of textile colorings and designs must be submitted when applying for this position. While gaining speed and experience as colorists, ambitious men and women look forward to moving up to the position of textile artist or textile designer.

Textile Designer

The textile designer has the opportunity to create original patterns or redesign already existing ones, while functioning concurrently as artist, colorist, and technician. It is just as important for the designer to know about new fibers and new machinery as it is to know about new styles and fashion trends. As the textile designer is responsible for creating and sketching ideas on paper and then translating them to fabrics, the ability to draw is an important asset in the designer's range of skills.

Textile artists may spend part of their workday viewing older fabrics and works of art, looking for ways to redo them as new fabric looks. Many firms have their own fabric libraries for this purpose. Museums are often excellent sources of inspiration for artists who can change or modify an old idea and give it a fresh new look that is both fashionable and marketable. In fact, many textile artists are able to create exciting new ideas simply by observing the world around them and being sensitive to trends, fads, and current events.

The textile designer also must acquire a technical background, as it is necessary to have knowledge of the capabilities and the limitations of the machinery used in the production of the fabric. This information broadens a designer's range and allows for the design of textiles that can be produced within a specific price category. The designer who is familiar with the latest changes in finishes, dyes, and equipment is often the most valuable to an employer.

Most colorist and design positions are full-time, but it may be possible for experienced colorist and textile artists to find free-lance work or short-term jobs that end once the assignment is completed. Because it takes a long time to build up free-lance clients and because employers expect highly professional work on short notice, it is never wise for beginners to consider free-lance assignments. One ought to have a minimum of six months of experience as a full-time colorist before giving serious consideration to a free-lance career.

Textile Stylist

Textile artists may want to consider another aspect of the textile field: textile styling. The stylist acts as a colorist, technician, merchandiser, salesperson, and occasionally even as a designer. This demanding and diversified job is for the person who has an extensive knowledge of the textile industry and who is fully aware of a wide range of fashion industry contacts and resources.

The stylist is responsible for determining the proper look, or *concept,* of the fabric line. The stylist may tell designers exactly what types of patterns to work on and may even indicate what colors are fashionable and should be used for new lines. The stylist then coordinates the efforts of the colorists and designers in the design studio with the efforts of the production workers at the mill or print plant, often many miles away. This may mean supervising or directing one or two or many more colorists and artists in the design studio. It also may mean frequent telephone contact with workers or supervisors at the plant where the fabric is being printed. The styling job also involves visits to the mill to check on the accuracy of the colors that are being printed. Unless the colors are exactly the ones ordered by the customer, hundreds of yards of fabric worth many thousands of dollars may by ruined. An alert stylist can prevent such expensive errors. Experienced textile artists also may be trained for this part of the production process at the plant, referred to as *mill work.* Having this sort of highly responsible "strike off" or mill work experience makes a textile worker very valuable to the employer.

Frequent contact with customers is important to learn what kinds of fabrics they wish to buy to produce their own products. It also is important to suggest ways in which the fabric can be used. This means working closely with a company's merchandising department to plan ahead for future lines.

Stylists may rely on the direction and advice of fabric editors or fabric coordinators who work for trade publications, fashion magazines, or industry associations. These fabric specialists have firsthand knowledge of texture, colors, and cloth construction and can provide stylists with information on new developments. The stylist's own good taste and fashion sense combined with researching the marketplace, referring to established trade resources, and many years of textile industry experience all work together to allow the stylist to predict what the public will want to buy a year or more in the future. The ability to do this season after season makes a textile stylist a success.

The stylist has the overwhelming responsibility of handling the fabric line from its beginning stages and seeing it through to completion. In knit firms, stylists are required to have a more technical background and work very closely with technicians in developing new yarns, or work with new kinds of yarns from the fiber companies. They may need to be very familiar with the latest advances in dyeing and finishing goods and still be responsible for styling new lines, coordinating colors, working with customers, and advising their customers on trends. In addition they have mill responsibility, and may even have a hand in designing and originating new patterns.

These styling opportunities are all highly desirable, very competitive, and generally pay well. The sales and profits of textile firms depend greatly on the talents of the stylist, and it is often a position reached only after many years of exposure in the textile field. Large textile manufacturing firms may hire several stylists, each one responsible for a specific group of fabrics, such as those used for home furnishings, children's wear, men's wear, or women's wear items.

Assistant Stylist

The stylist's assistant is really a person who is being trained to function as a stylist at some time in the future. The assistant can observe and learn a great deal on the job. Assistants help the stylist by setting up appointments with customers, having regular contact with the mills to check on the production process or to investigate particular problems, handling all the many clerical details and correspondence, and generally filling the shoes of the busy stylist in her or his absence.

These assistant spots are often filled by people who have completed college-level programs in textile design, textile technology, or fabric styling and who may have experience as a textile colorist or textile artist.

It is interesting to note that, with solid preparation in textile design, creative artists can branch out into other aspects of the design field: greeting card design; rug and carpet design; vinyl and wall covering design; lace, embroidery and applique design; and other related industries.

TEXTILE PRODUCTION

Textile production involves the many positions on the more technical side of today's high-tech textile industry. The duties and responsibilities of textile technologists are changing rapidly and opening exciting new vistas. Sophisticated new machinery produces vast quantities of fabric for a wide variety of uses. Men and women with technical training in specialized textile programs may begin careers as assistants in converting, quality control, and lab testing.

The demand for textiles is expected to increase over the next decade, as there is a growing need for new varieties of textile products in the apparel and home furnishing industries. Competition from foreign imports also may diminish, because international trade agreements now limit many imports. Overall, the numerous areas of work in the textile production field suggest a solid career choice for you to consider.

Textile Converter

In the process of making cloth, fibers are turned into yarns and yarns into fabrics. Who is responsible for the many decisions needed during this complex process? A person known as the textile converter decides what fibers to use, what width and weight of fabric to weave, and how many yards of the goods should be manufactured. The converter is the key person in this process, and he or she must be aware of all the needs of the customers.

The converter's job is to calculate the amount of fabric that will be bought, decide on certain finishes and dyes, and set prices. Large textile firms may employ many converters, each being a specialist in a certain fabric range for a particular market. The converter needs to know what is current in the marketplace, needs to keep in touch with customers, and must be able to quickly sum up new economic trends. The converter also must set the quality standards for various fabrics, depending on how that fabric will be used. Textiles purchased by a manufacturer of children's clothing require more strength and durability than a delicate chiffon fabric used for a woman's scarf. The converter plans the fabric construction and chooses a suitable finish based on the particular item's function. This ensures wearability and keeps the price at a reasonable level.

Assistant Converter

Assistants to the converter, as well as the converter, must be good at details and recordkeeping, be organized, and have excellent ability in handling figures, communicating with others, and working under pressure. Assistants help the converter keep tabs on the various processes of turning uncolored woven goods into finished fabric. This means the assistant converter must be familiar with all the necessary dyeing, printing, and finishing procedures. Assistants are responsible for keeping very accurate production and inventory records and for handling many other clerical duties. They also must help with establishing prices. This is known as *costing the fabric,* based on all the costs involved plus a margin of profit. There is heavy telephone work, and often telex communications for off-shore contacts when dealing with the textile mills and with customers who are always eager to learn about the status of the fabric they have ordered.

Men and women who have completed a two-year textile technology program can qualify for positions as assistant converters. More and more employers welcome graduates of four-year textile technology programs as well. Such specialized college-level programs offer courses in textile science, woven and knit fabrics, converting and costing, textile chemistry and dyeing, color analysis, textile testing, marketing principles, mathematics, and other related areas.

Lab Technician

A person trained in a textile technology program is equipped to perform tests in a laboratory to make sure that yarns, cloth, and clothing meet certain minimum acceptable requirements of wear. As consumers, we need to know that the garments and textiles we buy will not fade, shrink, or wear out too soon. Independent laboratories hire lab testers to perform these tests, as do fabric and garment manufacturers. Employers of lab technicians seek people who are able to organize their own work, as often the job requires the tester to work alone in a small laboratory setting. It is important to be able to follow precise instructions, enjoy detail work, and have the ability to write accurate and thorough reports of the result of each test performed. Lab testers handle a variety of simple equipment and chemicals, as well as more complicated equipment that can reveal how well an article of clothing is made or how strong and durable certain fabrics are. Lab technicians may be hired by independent testing laboratories or work directly for large manufacturers such as J.C. Penney or Sears.

Quality Control Trainee

Men and women training to fill quality control positions learn to examine and inspect fibers, yarns, cloth, and garments. They check to see that precise production standards and specifications are met. For example, if a garment has not been cut to the proper size, the customer will be unhappy and feel that the manufacturer has cheated the public. A hole or imperfection in a bolt of fabric or a variation of color in a piece of cloth prevents the sale of that item. Quality control trainees learn to identify these and other production-related problems at different stages of the manufacturing process and are asked to write reports based on their findings. Men and women with good analytical skills who enjoy detail and follow-up work and who have completed a textile technology program or an apparel production program are sought by employers for this position.

"NEVER IN NEW YORK"

When Lyn was in junior high school in Massachusetts, her parents encouraged her to start thinking about her future and plan for a career. Although her mother was a seamstress, Lyn had no special feeling for sewing or designing. She remembers that the fashion buying area seemed "somewhat glamorous" to her when she was taking distributive education courses in high school.

Interested in furthering her education, she applied to a variety of colleges in the Boston area. Having no interest in living or studying in New York, she applied to the Fashion Institute of Technology only as a back-up school. She was accepted at every one of the colleges she applied to, and FIT's acceptance was the last one to come in the mail. She remembers knowing that, despite its New York location, FIT was going to be her choice!

Based on her knowledge of merchandising gained in high school classes, she chose to major in fashion buying and merchandising. After settling in and talking to some students who were textile majors, Lyn became interested in learning more about that area. Talking to the chairperson of the textile technology department gave her a great deal of career-related information to think about, and after careful consideration she changed her major. She had a rather individualized program that took advantage of her early interest in the merchandising field and her new-found interest in textiles.

Thinking back about her schooling, Lyn feels that every single course she took was important, as she has used all of the technical information she acquired at different times in her career. She even discovered which areas were not of special interest to her and were better for her to avoid.

Lyn was eager to start the job-hunting process as she neared the end of her two-year textile technology program. Her placement counselor helped her arrange an interview with a major textile manufacturing company. One open job was listed as a production assistant, but turned out to have too much clerical detail to interest Lyn. However, the personnel interviewer who spoke with Lyn was quite impressed with her background and her abilities and promised to keep her in mind for other opportunities as they arose in the firm. And the interviewer did exactly that, contacting Lyn when a sales position in one of the company's divisions became available.

Lyn went through a long series of interviews, ten in all. And the very last one was held on the morning of her graduation. With her cap and gown in hand, she was asked to identify and describe various fabrics, discuss the construction of different weaves, and talk about dyeing and finishing processes with the interviewer. The position was available because a very experienced salesperson was retiring after thirty years of employment with the company. The interviewer was impressed with Lyn but had some reservations about a nineteen-year-old filling such a demanding sales spot. Many textile firms are quite conservative and not at all used to such young women in the sales area, though this situation is rapidly changing. But despite whatever misgivings they may have had, Lyn made it clear that she could handle the job and that she was very interested in the position. And she was hired!

As a sales trainee for the wholesale home furnishings division of the textile company, Lyn began her assignment by running errands, making coffee, folding sample pieces of material, and getting exposure in every area of the showroom. After just one week at work, she started to see a few customers—something very unusual for any sales trainee. After six months on the job, and her first raise, her duties changed. She was asked to take on more responsibilities, such as showing the company's line of textiles to the trade newspapers. She began to work closely with home fashion editors of magazines and assisted them in choosing fabrics for various made-to-measure items like pillows and cushions.

The sales showroom accommodates the company's customers—mainly retailers—when they are on buying trips in New York City and cannot be serviced by the regular "outside" salesperson. Lyn enjoyed this service role and liked learning how to put together presentations and displays of merchandise for the retailers' stores. She coordinated a presentation of a new line of fabrics and pillows for all the employees in the showroom to familiarize them with the latest items in the line. It was a great success. Less than a year later, Lyn was the assistant showroom manager. Now her job was to see that everything for the large showroom was attractively displayed, that displays were changed regularly, and that all samples were always in stock for the customers. She handled customer problems and trained new showroom staff. Lyn describes the job as "seeing that the showroom ran smoothly—definitely not a glamour job!"

While working hard to manage all aspects of the showroom, Lyn discovered that a position was available as an assistant department head in the firm's pillow division. Her boss did not encourage her to apply for the job, wanting her to remain on the showroom floor. But Lyn was convinced that she should apply for the spot. She wanted to work in a smaller unit and learn the total operation of the merchandising, marketing, and administration areas.

After spending two and a half weeks meeting with her boss and explaining why the move would be a good one for her and for the firm, Lyn succeeded in selling herself for the job. Now, working with two other associates, Lyn has the feeling she is part of a small group venture. She has the task of buying piece goods for pillows and importing ready-made pillows. She is working closely with two plants in Massachusetts and Connecticut and makes occasional trips to those plants as production problems come up. Two times a year, major production programs are scheduled by Lyn and her two colleagues. She has heavy customer contact and, in addition to servicing her major accounts, acts as advisor and consultant to the outside sales staff, who relies on her for news of fashion and home furnishings trends.

Lyn is eager to move ahead. She hopes her future duties will allow her closer contact with the large retail stores that buy her pillows, and that will surely mean more travel and more responsibility for her. Her parents are very proud of her. Their daughter, who once shunned the big city, is now an important part of one of its major industries. And Lyn's future is bright. She knows she has come a long way in a field that presents endless opportunities for someone with her vitality and drive.

CHAPTER 4

FASHION MERCHANDISING

If you would like to become one of the fast-moving and energetic people who choose the fashion items that we will be shopping for in the seasons to come, you might consider the positions of showroom salesperson, fashion buyer, and fashion merchandiser. You can find these jobs offered in thousands of stores located all over the country. Jobs are available in boutiques, department stores, specialty stores, wholesalers' and manufacturers' showrooms, buying offices, and discount shops that sell fashion-related items. What's more, the growing focus on fashion has created a real need for trained people in the fashion merchandising field. Retailers, large and small, are expanding their fashion departments, which, of course, puts a greater demand on the production capacity of manufacturers.

Retailing, often called the heartbeat of the national economy, is an industry defined by new technology and new products, good skills, and marketing savvy. There is a renewed sense of vitality in the world of retailing, as a result of recent mergers, diversificatiions, and growth in new products. These developments point to interesting employment opportunities for the future. Retailing continues to offer dynamic careers with the challenge of planning for the ongoing changes. The trick, of course, is to make sure millions of dollars of the appropriate merchandise is in the right place at the right time.

The fact that retail outlets are so numerous throughout this country makes beginning career opportunities in this field more available than in the wholesale and manufacturing areas. Retailing experience is extremely important in its own right, but also as a stepping-stone to more advanced merchandising careers. In some areas, in fact, it is often a definite requirement for a beginning position. But wholesalers and manufacturing companies also offer entry-level jobs in which the employee has the opportunity to learn the ins and outs of an extremely important part of the world of fashion.

What is this world all about? Merchandising is simply the selection and purchasing of merchandise from the manufacturer and the selling of that merchandise to the customer. Needless to say, it must be done in the most efficient and profitable way possible. Merchandising activities are really the heart of any retail store. And these principles of merchandising can be learned. But aside from special training there are certain character traits that also are essential for a successful career in one of the many phases of the merchandising field. For example, it is important to be outgoing and well-organized. Energy and stamina are essential, as is the ability to get along well with other people and work under stress. Good leadership abilities and self-confidence are very important. And in this field there's no overlooking excellent grooming and a sense of fashion. An ability to handle figures and details is also a necessary ingredient for the person who wants to enter this fascinating, fast-changing world.

In fashion merchandising, you can expect to work long hours, but such hard work does not go unrewarded. Among your benefits are adventure, recognition, a chance to see the direct results of your efforts, advancement, and competitive financial compensation.

Are you generally interested in all areas of fashion—from the newest looks in clothing to cosmetics to home furnishings? Are you easy to deal with and do you enjoy working with people on a daily basis? Can you express yourself well and do you enjoy public contact? Do you find the changes in trends and fashion looks exciting? What about adventure? Are you willing to explore new market items—checking out trends and meeting the many new people involved in creating the latest fashions? Action is a large part of this world—it operates at a fast tempo, so the people in it must move quickly and think quickly. If you are prepared to work really hard and tolerate long hours, pressures, deadlines, and competition, the dynamic world of fashion merchandising may hold a career for you.

Merchandising is big business, and unlike some segments of the fashion industry, it isn't limited geographically. Chances are you can find a fashion-oriented retail store just about anywhere in the country— from a large city to a shopping mall in your neighborhood. And fashion is now an important part of the total merchandising picture, because more and more it has become of concern to us all. No longer is fashion solely the domain of the wealthy, as technological developments have made sophisticated styles available to even the most modest of budgets. And it is these styles, as well as those that cater to people who can afford more extravagant wardrobes, that will be your concern as a fashion merchandiser.

GETTING STARTED

The quickest way to get started and provide yourself with the best all-around training for a career in merchandising is to get a selling job. Summer or part-time work in sales is fine. Even a temporary job during the busy Christmas season will give you a wide variety of experience and a taste of this fast-moving industry. Retailing is a whole lot more than just ringing up sales behind a counter. It involves all activities associated with the sale, such as: displaying the product; pricing, distributing, promoting, and advertising the item; dealing with customers; and training and supervising the work force. Customer relations is probably the most important item on this varied list of a retailer's duties. Don't underestimate the value of your sales experience! It will put you in direct contact with the customer and give you the chance to gain product knowledge and to learn about stock routines and records. You will learn how to work a cash register, make change, write up sales tickets, and handle refunds and C.O.D. sales. You may have a chance to arrange new merchandise on the shelves or set up counter displays. You also may discover what items people are buying and why. And most important, you will learn what things you should and should not say about the goods you are trying to sell.

Don't turn down a stock job either! You can be valuable to the retail store by keeping track of what items have sold and, by filling those empty shelves, help the salespeople to make the sale. You also may be able to help with special orders or even ticket the merchandise as it comes into the stockroom from the manufacturer or wholesaler. Keeping accurate records of the movement of all the goods in the stockroom may be part of your experience, too.

Stock and sales jobs may be available to you while you are still in school. Sales jobs offer excellent experience to anyone interested in the retail field. If your are really interested in a career in merchandising you must consider a two- or four-year program in merchandising, retailing, or related areas to allow you to move up and compete for the full-time jobs in the industry once you are ready for them. You will be prepared for those jobs with courses that may include fashion marketing, sales promotion, fashion buying, merchandise math, consumer motivation, merchandise planning, retail operations, product knowledge, human resources, management, computers for business, advertising and promotion, business law, small store management, and others that are offered by colleges that have specialized programs. Be sure to look into colleges that provide a work study or co-op program that allows you to work in some aspect of the industry and observe it firsthand as part of the merchandising curriculum. Experience in any retail store is valuable to you and the skills you acquire are transferable. Once trained in retailing procedures, you can switch from a large operation to a smaller one, from a discount chain to a department store, from a store in New York City to one in California. There are shops and manufacturers everywhere. You might even think of opening your own store someday!

HOW DID IT ALL BEGIN?

Retailers have been providing products to customers as long as there has been a society in which to buy and sell. We know that trade in marketplaces existed in early Egypt, Greece, and Rome thousands of years ago. However, department stores as we now know them began only about one hundred years ago.

The growth of America's cities caused modern-day retailing to blossom. People moved to the cities from rural areas and began to rely upon merchants for food, clothing, and other necessities. In retailing's early stages, the merchants often were artisans who made their own products. Some sold their own items and also bought and sold the items of other artisans and thus developed a larger trade.

As laborers left their farms for the cities and more European immigrants began to arrive in this country, American cities grew by leaps and bounds. By 1880 New York City had a population of two million people, Philadelphia nearly one million, and Chicago a half million people—all needing and wanting goods.

As the country's needs changed with its shifting population, so a new kind of retailer was called for. In 1859 the Great Atlantic and Pacific Tea Company opened its first retail store, and twenty years later F. W. Woolworth opened his first "dime store." All over the nation general stores also cropped up. The general store owner carried a wide variety of items and was really a merchandiser. The owner knew exactly which items were in stock and knew all of the customers and what they wanted to buy. Not many years later, Montgomery Ward and Sears Roebuck set up the country's two largest mail-order houses, which allowed customers to order a wide variety of merchandise through the mail.

A new type of store developed in the larger cities: the department store, which opened to supply the needs of the growing number of city dwellers. Soon it became clear that as the nation's population grew, so too would the retailing world. Years later, when the automobile became as much a part of life as the department store, retail stores began opening parking lots to accommodate customer's cars. And then, as more and more people gave up the congestion of the cities and started to move to the suburbs, something else happened: the stores had to go where the customers were. All across the United States, branch stores of large downtown department stores were built. Some of the branches were even larger and more modern than the parent store. Thus, suburban shopping centers and malls came into being. Generally, the main store has retained the management offices and still offers the widest array of merchandise. However, the branch store is now an accepted and important part of the retail world and very much a part of your territory as a merchandiser.

RETAILING

Selling is what the retail business is all about. America's greatness in producing a huge variety of merchandise would be meaningless if that merchandise were not sold. By knowing the needs of the customer and then letting the manufacturer know those needs by placing orders for specific items, retailers can make sure the right goods are available at the right time and price. But the retailer also needs imagination to think of new merchandising ideas that will encourage sales. Thus, the retailer keeps an eye and ear on trends and style changes and must be sensitive to the customer's requests at all times.

Until recently, retailing was not considered a prestige career. But times have changed! Retailing now appeals to growing numbers of bright and hard-working young men and women, eager to make their mark in this creative and exciting profession. The growth and appeal of the retail industry has been so challenging that young adults would be foolish not to think of it as an exciting career option.

The retailing industry is one of the largest employers of workers in the United States. It is likely that as much as fifty percent of our work force is involved in some aspect of retail activity. And more and more of the brightest and best of our college graduates are selecting retailing as their career choice.

STORES

Stores exist in all shapes and sizes—from the very large to a one-person operation—and flourish in every part of the country. Most people in the retailing field actually work in the stores. Some of these stores are independently owned, while others are part of large chain store operations. Although each store you are familiar with has its own image and appeal, chances are it falls into one of these major categories: the department store, the specialty store, the mass merchandising chain store, and the discount store. These four kinds of stores exemplify the world of retailing in the United States, and together they present countless opportunities for beginners with an interest in some aspect of retailing.

The Department Store. A department store offers for sale everything you might want under one roof. The biggest ones carry any item you can imagine for children, men, and women. In addition, they have a vast selection of goods for the home: furniture, washing machines, food items, records, books, toys, and garden equipment. Sometimes there is even a pharmacy or an automotive department where you can buy tires for the family car! In many department stores, you can buy everything from birdseed to gourmet cheese in one stop. Not every department store's offerings are this varied, but most offer a fine assortment of soft goods—clothing and accessories—and hard goods—appliances, tools, sporting goods, and similar items. Certainly a selection varied enough to satisfy most of our shopping needs.

The Specialty Store. Specialty stores also come in many sizes. They can be quite large with several branch stores, or very small and specialize in just one type of merchandise. Specialty stores generally carry fashion apparel and accessories. Some will offer items for all ages and both sexes. Others specialize even further in selling only women's clothing or just infant's wear or fine jewelry. The important feature is that specialty stores do not carry any hard goods-no furniture or equipment that would put them in the department store category. Some specialty stores are single shops, individually owned with rather small staffs. They often are referred to as "momma and poppa" stores. The others are a part of a larger organization and may be centrally managed. But they all have a very specialized group of items for sale.

The Chain Store. The 1920s and 1930s brought us the idea of chain stores, and they are still thriving today. Chain stores are centrally owned and their many branches may be found in several cities and states. Some chain operations are large enough to have stores all across the country. Some chain stores, such as Sears and J.C. Penney, are probably familiar names to you. Sears even has stores in foreign countries. It is a world-wide retail chain, with 400,000 workers. Not all chain stores carry an enormous variety of merchandise, but they all offer the same items at similar prices all across the nation.

The Discount Store. The discount store is a relatively new retailing idea that became popular after World War II. Some are specialty discount stores, featuring only apparel and accessories. Others resemble department stores and offer a broad range of goods. The discount store may be a single store or part of a small or large chain.

The real appeal of these stores for shoppers is that discount operations offer bargains, often on well-known brands of merchandise. To allow for this, discounters work on low markups and low expenses. This usually means low rents and a minimum of special services, such as gift wrapping or charge accounts. But it also means a savings for the customers, and a bargain has great appeal for everyone.

THERE'S WORK TO BE DONE IN THE STORES

It takes a great many kinds of skills and a wide assortment of highly motivated people to keep America's retail world alive. This means that there is a broad range of job possibilities for anyone with an interest in retailing.

In general, it is true that the larger the store, the greater are the executive and supervisory opportunities. In smaller shops, the owner and one or two workers may handle everything: planning, buying, receiving, pricing, advertising, displaying, wrapping, selling, and even keeping accounts and inventory records. In a store employing hundreds of workers, however, different tasks are assigned to workers in different departments. Executives and supervisors are needed to direct the work of each unit.

You must be ready to devote long hours, including evenings and weekends, as a beginner. Entry-level workers are required to work these hours to progress to the next level. Be prepared to experience everything from the stockroom to receiving and shipping of goods. If you are entrepeneurial and enjoy the idea of selecting and selling merchandise, retailing may be just right for you. You'll be on the move, have a chance to travel, and work with many different people. You'll also have the chance to see the results of your decisions rather quickly. And for many, that is very gratifying!

Most large retailing firms offer an executive training program for men and women with specialized college backgrounds to groom them for executive positions in the future.

EXECUTIVE TRAINING PROGRAMS

As the general level of education continues to rise and more students receive college degrees, it is truly important to think in terms of preparing yourself with as much education and training as possible. Major department stores offer an ideal but demanding first job to those interested in a career in fashion merchandising—the executive training program. A four-year college degree is essential for landing a place in such a training program, although some programs may consider exceptional two-year graduates with strong school and work experience. These competitive and highly desirable assignments mean you have been selected because of your potential executive ability. Most executive trainees in retailing are groomed for careers as buyers, although there are other career paths as well.

The store that hires you for its executive training program will groom you in all aspects of merchandising and develop your management skills. People hired for executive training programs are carefully selected from four-year colleges and schools offering master's degrees in business management and retailing.

While competing for a slot in an executive training program, candidates are closely scrutinized. Often store representatives interview students on college campuses and then invite them to visit their stores for additional interviews. They are evaluated on how they look, how they present themselves, their past school and work records, how enthusiastic and energetic they seem, and on how much interest they show for the fashion merchandising area.

Once hired, the group of beginners starts a rigorous on-the-job training program that often includes evening and weekend work. The length of the program depends upon the training policy of each store. Executive training programs often begin in the summer, after graduation. Some stores add additional groups in September or in February. This is a paid assignment and trainees begin earning a salary the day they report for work. In the first weeks, they may visit all the store branches and learn as much as possible about the divisions within them. They will meet the members of the management team and perhaps even the chairperson of the board and the president of the firm. They will hear each of the managers talk about her or his division and how it operates and how all the areas of the store work together. Of course, they will be trained in selling procedures and will spend some time right on the selling floor. Once assigned to a particular department, the trainees will have a chance to meet the buyer and the assistant buyer and observe how they operate. They may also find themselves transferred to several different selling departments so that they may get many different kinds of merchandising experiences.

Part of the training period will be spent in areas such as the operations division, working side by side with employees in the receiving room or the shipping department; or in the control division, observing the billing process or the auditing team. Somewhere between six and twelve months of training and, depending upon how quickly jobs become available, the trainee may be ready for an assignment as an assistant buyer. This could be a position in the main store or in one of the branches.

Throughout the executive program, the trainee's performance is evaluated by the personnel or human resources department. Progress and productivity are noted, and the supervisors and training director review each trainee's performance. This kind of evaluation is an ongoing process.

Although each store's executive training program tries to groom its members for executive positions in the future, they all operate a bit differently. In some stores, it is typical for a trainee to land a buyer's job after about two years with the store. In other cases, it may take much longer. Depending upon the employer, the amount of time spent in the training program will vary, as will the number of weeks spent on each assignment.

Executive training programs offer a splendid beginning for a fashion merchandising career, but certainly they are not for everyone. If this type of initiation into merchandising does not appeal to you, there are still many other ways of starting your career. But first, pinpoint your area of interest. For example, try to decide where you may feel the most comfortable: in a large or small store, in a chain store, a specialty shop, a discount operation, or a department store. Learn as much as you can about each of these stores and investigate the career opportunities they can offer you.

THE FUNCTIONS OF RETAILING

The function of any retail operation is basically the same, whether large or small. Tasks performed by one or two workers in a small retail store must be handled by a greater number of people in a large store, but in essence these tasks differ only in quantity, not in kind. Therefore, regardless of the size of store, we can talk of the five important functions of retailing which are essential to all operations. They are: *merchandising*— planning, buying, and selling goods; *sales promotion*—designing programs to help sell the goods and encourage customers to shop in the store; *store operations* or *store management*—providing services for the customers, maintaining the store, and ensuring the proper receiving, storing, and delivery of merchandise; *personnel*—training, placing, evaluating, and promoting employees; and *control*—keeping tabs of profits and losses and all the other financial details of the business.

Gaining experience in one of these areas will not limit you. Good work experience in any specialized field may lead to broader responsibilities later on in your career. Each of the five major areas can offer opportunities for your progress. However, the wide range of entry jobs within all five areas makes it impractical to offer a comprehensive list of opportunities within the limited space of this book. Therefore, let's focus specifically on the merchandising part of this fascinating business.

THE MERCHANDISE CLERK OR HEAD OF STOCK

This job can be an excellent starting point for you. Time is spent in the receiving and marking room, identifying the hundreds of items of merchandise that have been delivered by the manufacturers for sale in your department. The merchandise must be processed quickly and brought to the selling floors for immediate sale. Good record-keeping skills are a necessity in this position, as reports must be prepared quickly and accurately. The buyer decides whether to reorder based on information on the number of items sold each day. In most stores, electronic data processing equipment is now used to help collect this information for the buyer. Familiarity with a computer is an asset.

The merchandise clerk usually is responsible for keeping up-to-date inventory records on the stock that is handled daily. Also, if the clerk is responsible for the stock in the branch stores as well, he or she must maintain telephone contact with these stores to coordinate the shipping and receiving of the goods. Chances are there will be contact with salespeople, clerical workers from other branches, assistant buyers, and very close contact with the buyers of various departments.

The position of merchandise clerk is often the first rung on the career ladder and might be filled by a high school graduate who has been promoted from the selling floor. It is a good position for anyone in the midst of completing a specialized degree program in a community

THE MERCHANDISING DIVISION

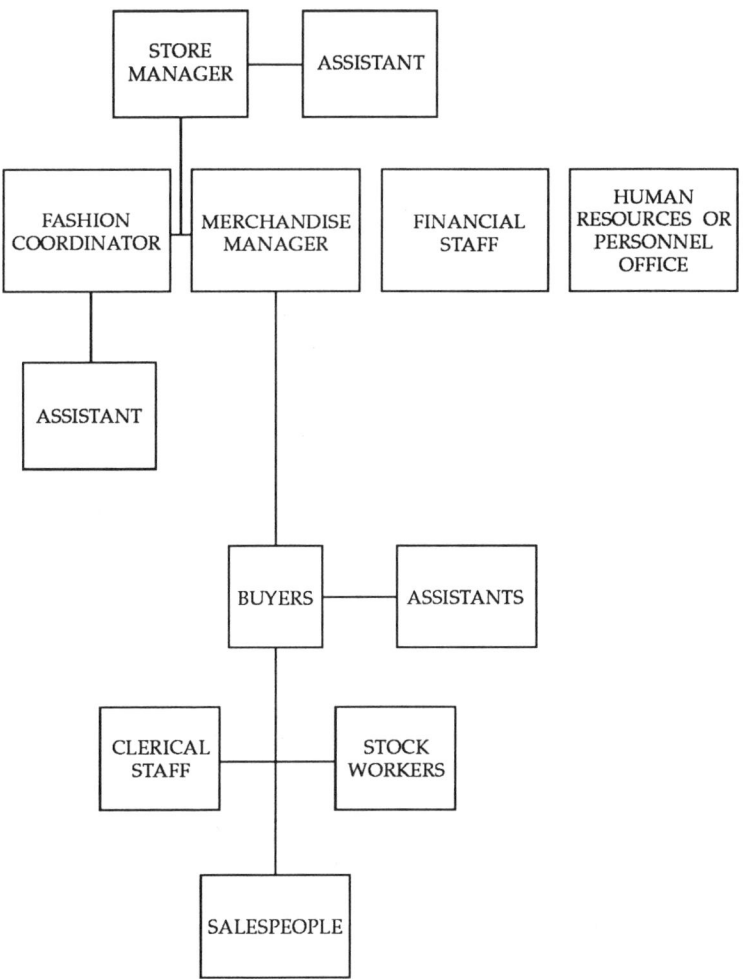

college or for someone waiting to enter an executive training program. The job of stock clerk may be one to consider for part-time or summer employment while you are still in school. The tons of merchandise that large stores receive must all be recorded, tagged, and distributed. Working under the direction of the head of stock, the stock clerk plays a large part in the prompt and successful completion of these important tasks.

ASSISTANT BUYER

The position of assistant buyer is the most important stepping-stone to becoming a buyer. It is often the position given to college graduates who complete an executive training program. Assistant buyers may truly be thought of as buyers-in-training. The position involves all-around exposure to each phase of the buyer's responsibilities, including all management duties. It includes handling some of the department's budget, selecting and promoting merchandise, maintaining sales and inventory records, and supervising sales and stock employees. It also means spending a good deal of time in the sales area with salespeople and customers, and becoming familiar with and knowledgeable about merchandise. The assistant buyer often must assume the more routine aspects of the buyer's job, but what wonderful on-the-job training this position offers!

The assistant buyer will learn how to present merchandise properly and how to handle promotions and special department events. He or she will frequently accompany the buyer on visits to manufacturers (referred to as vendors in the industry) in the search for new sources of merchandise. Assistants will often take charge of and run a department in the buyer's absence. An assistant buyer also may be in charge of some part of a department. For example, an assistant in a sportswear department may have full responsibility for skirts. In some stores, the term "associate buyer" is used to describe the person who has buying responsibility for a particular category of merchandise rather than for the entire department.

Assistant buyers have contact with salespeople, merchandise clerks, and stock workers, as well as with the promotion, publicity, and display departments. There also will be meetings to attend with other assistant buyers, which is an ongoing part of the store's training program. As you can see, the days are full and busy, but very rewarding. If the assistant buyer is working closely with a buyer who is also a good teacher, much will be learned. Stores need good buyers for the future, and a great deal of training and preparation is invested in each assistant buyer.

The next step involves the assistant buyer's ability to show some potential for the role of full buyer. Merchandise managers and training supervisors often have a part in deciding not only whether an assistant buyer has the potential to be promoted to buyer, but when that promotion should occur. It also is possible to advance from one buying area to another. Someone who has been a successful assistant in the sportswear department may be promoted to a buyer in the shoe department. Although the merchandise may be different, the skills and techniques needed to run a profitable department are the same.

THE BUYER OR DEPARTMENT HEAD

The key person in the merchandising process, and one of the most important and responsible jobs in the business is that of the buyer or department head. Selecting items that customers will want to buy and then determining if you were correct is very exciting. The buyer needs to find the merchandise customers want and sell it at a profit, while always being informed of the competition's offerings. If the merchandise doesn't sell, the buyer must figure out the reason: poor quality? wrong color? too expensive? The days of a successful buyer are filled with excitement, pressure, hard work, and plenty of satisfaction. Buyers often spend a great deal of time away from the store, visiting markets or sources of supplies where they search for items that will sell. Travel to showrooms and factories is involved in the important New York, Los Angeles, Chicago, and Dallas markets. Buyers for certain departments may travel the world—to Europe, the Orient, or South America. These varied activities mean constant competition and a direct responsibility for sales and profits. And behind the excitement of choosing merchandise always must be a great deal of sound business judgment.

Every buyer has a specialty. Some buy women's sportswear only, some buy men's overcoats and suits. In large retail stores, the buyer's responsibility may be even narrower; for example, buying only women's dresses in the moderate price range or buying only preteen clothing. The bigger the store is, the more buyers it needs and the more specialized are the duties of those buyers.

Buyers always must operate with certain key questions in mind: Who are the customers? Are they rural, urban, or suburban families? Do they want conservative clothing or very trendy and stylish items? Are they budget conscious or will they be able to spend freely on clothing, accessories, and home furnishings? And what kind of store are you buying for—a high fashion shop, a mass market operation, a discount chain?

When a buyer is given a budget for a particular department for a season, the process of deciding which items to buy from which manufacturers begins. This process includes contact with a manufacturer or wholesaler to view and select the line of items, agreeing upon a price and delivery date, setting the selling price of the items, supervising the sales staff, being aware of the stockroom situation, arranging for the return of improper or defective merchandise, marking down slow-moving items, and helping to promote, display, and advertise those items. Buyers need complete knowledge of the customer's likes and dislikes, of the store's policies, and of resources or vendors.

The buyer, as the head of a department, has many of the responsibilities of an individual store owner, and can likewise measure her or his success in dollars and cents of profit for that particular department. They

constantly compete against their own records and those of other departments and other stores. Every buyer tries to make this season's profits
better than those of last season.

The buyer also needs to spend some time on the sales floor. This
means having some contact with both customers and salespeople. In this
way, the buyer can learn which items are selling, what needs to be
reordered, what customers are asking for, and what items need to be
marked down for quick sale.

All this information, plus information gathered from reading fashion
journals and magazines and from shopping in other stores, comprises
an integral part of the buyer's carefully thought-out plan for running the
department profitably. Buyers also need to acquaint the sales staff with
all new merchandise. Meetings are held to tell the salespeople about
certain features of the merchandise and to encourage them to pass that
news on to the customers. Important buying decisions are discussed
with the buyer's boss, the merchandise manager.

Despite numerous precautions, don't think that buyers never make
mistakes! Clearance racks often tell us that the buyer miscalculated
some factor concerning the merchandise that customers were supposed
to buy like hotcakes. If goods don't sell, a buyer may try to get an
outside jobber to buy some of the merchandise. The jobber may want to
buy the goods at a reduced price and then resell them. Or the buyer may
try to arrange a special promotion or sale on the items to attract the
customers' attention. The last resort is to put the merchandise on
"clearance," which means reducing the price drastically to encourage
very quick sales. Obviously, buyers try not to have too many items on
the clearance racks, because it lowers the department's profits. Buyers
also must spend some time figuring out what went wrong and why the
goods did not sell well. The buyer must be aware when slow-selling
items seem to come from the same manufacturer, and the buyer may not
want to buy from that company in the future.

The opposite of the slow-moving product situation is known as "the
runner." A runner is an item that really catches on. It is a fast seller and

may need to be reordered many times. To keep up with the customers' demands, it may be reordered for the next season in different colors or in different fabrics.

Buyers must work well with figures. Profits and losses are always expressed in dollars and cents, and the buyer of every department must be proficient in math in order to compute the daily sales, margins, markdowns, and inventories. These daily computations enable buyers to plan their budgets and examine their profits and thus measure their success or failure on a day-to-day basis. No wonder good math skills are so important, even with the help of calculators and computers. Most buyers learn to work with computer printouts as a means of quickly identifying their department's daily tallies.

It should be easy to see that much of the fun and stimulation of the buyer's job comes from the variety, diversity, and challenge of each new day's work. Successful buyers may be rewarded with increased earnings, and by being given responsibility for a larger department or several departments. These achievements are realized only after years of work as a buyer. Before this you must undergo training as an assistant buyer, a position that can last anywhere from two to six years, depending on the policy of the store and your own capability and potential. Once you have been made a full buyer, you can be certain you have demonstrated a good deal of know-how in your area of specialization.

THE MERCHANDISE MANAGER

After you have learned the demanding job of buying for one and perhaps several departments, you may become one of the talented people promoted to the position of merchandise manager. The merchandise manager is directly responsible for a group of buyers and in many ways functions as a consultant, teacher, director, guidance counselor, and mentor. Merchandise managers must share the knowledge they have gained over the years with their buyers. They have complete control of the amounts of money their buyers will be spending and therefore attempt to guide the buyers on adventurous yet profitable paths. Merchandise managers work closely with the store's other merchandise managers and also compete with them for a larger share of customers' sales. And as with every buyer, beating last season's sales and profit figures is the merchandise manager's goal.

New shops within the store, boutiques, or special departments may be the result of a creative merchandise manager's thinking. They may add glamour, a slightly different approach, or a brand-new outlook to the division. For those who have the urge to make a division's business grow as if it were their own, and who possess an adventurous and enterprising spirit, it would be worthwhile to consider the position of merchandise manager, once the other required steps are completed.

Merchandise managers need to work very closely with buyers to help them in planning their visits to various markets and to teach them to turn their sales into profits. They must be familiar with each of the departments within their division. They must be aware of all new manufacturers and suppliers and alert buyers to new items, ideas, and trends that may have a bearing on sales. They also must continue to search out new and different sources, which may mean as much traveling as they did when they were buyers. The demands on their time and knowledge are great, but the rewards are often greater than the effort put forth. Besides, there is the opportunity to train support staff made up of buyers, assistants, merchandise clerks, and salespeople to work toward a profitable and exciting division. No small consideration for the true professional!

FASHION COORDINATOR

One of the most competitive, glamorous, and sought-after jobs in the world of retailing is that of the fashion coordinator. Just as the title implies, the fashion coordinator has to make sure that all fashion departments are kept up-to-date on the latest fashion trends. Fashion coordinators are taste makers and should have a highly developed sense of fashion themselves. The fashion coordinator advises buyers and merchandise managers on style trends, assists the advertising and promotion departments, and handles fashion shows. This last responsibility involves choosing clothing and accessories, working with the models, and arranging for publicity.

The fashion coordinator also may work with local high schools and colleges to form a "college board" or similar fashion event. The coordinator often will go into wholesale and retail markets to get the feel of what is happening in the fashion world and relay the information gathered on these trips to store employees to keep them well informed. Fashion coordinators also may suggest what merchandise from other departments might be offered in a single shop or boutique. In this way, the coordinator attempts to present a single fashion look or "fashion story" to the customer, so that buyers in each department don't end up with conflicting looks for each season. For example, the fashion coordinator will work hard to ensure that there will be shoes, handbags, jewelry, and cosmetics to coordinate with the sportswear and dresses being promoted in different areas of the store.

The job is a busy one, but a very desirable one. Knowledge of fashion merchandising and broad retail experience are required, plus imagination and a highly developed fashion sense. Sensitivity to what is new and ahead of the times is vital, as is an interest in color, design, style, and fabrics. Of course, the fashion coordinator must look and sound the part as well by being a model of stylish dress, good grooming, and excellent speaking ability.

With the recent focus on fashion in the home, it is likely that a fashion coordinator will be an expert not only in the clothing and accessories areas but also in coordinating merchandise in the home furnishings departments. It may fall to the fashion coordinator to put together a group of model rooms, using the latest styles of furniture, fabrics, and accessories. Many customers enjoy viewing these model rooms, as they inspire them to consider new ways of decorating their own homes or apartments.

If this job interests you, remember that it is highly competitive, and job openings tend to be scarce. Unless you are a top-notch candidate with an extensive merchandising background, it may be an extremely difficult or even impossible career to achieve. In addition to stores, jobs for fashion coordinators may be found in advertising agencies and textile and clothing manufacturing firms.

ASSISTANT TO THE FASHION COORDINATOR

The entry-level job for anyone who dreams of becoming a fashion coordinator is assistant to the fashion coordinator. The assistant may be hired in any type of retail store, buying office, textile firm, pattern company, or manufacturer's office. Or sometimes a trade organization may have need for such a beginner. The duties are often clerical in nature, and for this job good typing skills are an important asset. There is a great deal of detail and follow-up work that the fashion coordinator delegates to the assistant, such as making appointments, telephoning contacts, booking models, and even running errands. But it is possible for the assistant to work closely with the fashion coordinator in putting on fashion shows, helping to write fashion bulletins, and spending time out in the market observing trends and new looks.

To compete successfully for these very scarce and very competitive beginning jobs, it is essential to look the part of a fashion coordinator-to-be. Excellent grooming and a keen sense of fashion are required. Poise, a polished manner, and a good speaking voice are all part of the personal qualities that will be looked for. To stand in for and represent the fashion coordinator successfully, the assistant must be a model of good taste and style. And, of course, clerical skills and good typing are a plus.

THE STORE MANAGER

The broad title of store manager has many duties attached to it. As chain and specialty stores continue to grow and add new branches, it is a job increasingly available to those who would like to run the store—perhaps even their own stores in the future. The store manager is in charge of every aspect of the store's operation: opening and closing the store, serving customers, bringing daily receipts to the bank, keeping the store supplied with merchandise, hiring and training workers, and handling the displays, advertising, accounts, and store security. This job focuses on every phase of retailing. If the store being managed is a large one, many assistants work with the manager. In small outlets, the store manager is a one-person show, handling everything in an attempt to help the store grow and become more profitable.

ASSISTANT STORE MANAGER

Department stores, boutiques, chain stores, and specialty stores need mature and dependable individuals to groom for store managers. Starting out as an assistant store manager, you work closely with the store manager and assist in all store operations as described here. Working as a salesperson may be a part of the assignment as well. The training is generally informal and occurs on-the-job rather than in a classroom situation. As in any retail operation, you must be prepared for late evenings and some weekend work. With good experience, it is possible to be promoted to the position of store manager once you have proved yourself.

Those who would like to rise to this position must have initiative, a high energy level, leadership abilities, the capacity to deal with many people in a firm yet friendly manner, and a good fashion sense. The ability to relocate also may figure importantly in your success, as chain stores may place employees in any area where jobs open up. In suburban areas, a car is often required.

RESIDENT BUYING OFFICES
AND CENTRAL BUYING OFFICES

If the retail store operation has no special appeal for you and you live in an area where there are buying offices, you might consider working in a resident buying office or in a central buying office. Both are an excellent source of entry-level jobs for people starting out in fashion merchandising. And, as resident buying offices and central buying offices have a five-day work week and are not open on evenings or weekends, they often have greater appeal for those who want to avoid the long and irregular hours of most retail operations.

Resident Buying Offices

Resident buying offices service stores and shops all across the country. Since most manufacturers have their showrooms in New York City, it is hard for smaller stores outside the New York area to keep pace with the heartbeat of the fashion market. So these stores, chains, and mail-order houses work with a resident buying office. Resident buying offices are really misnamed. Their true function is not one of buying at all, but of giving service to their customers. Resident buying offices help their stores' buyers do a better job of buying. They offer out-of-town buyers all of these services: covering wholesale markets and reporting on trends; buying for the member stores if requested; following up on deliveries, adjustments, and complaints about merchandise; providing office space, clerical help, and mail and telephone service for visiting buyers; going with the out-of-town buyers to the market; suggesting sales promotion and publicity ideas; getting merchandise samples for the buyer to see before buying decisions are made; planning merchandise clinics or previews of the leading resources; and offering fashion coordination services.

Resident buying offices are located mainly in New York City, the fashion market of the country. A smaller group of offices is located in the Los Angeles area. Some resident buying offices are owned by a group of stores, while others are independently owned to offer their services to stores for a fee. Either way, the resident buying office is staffed with employees who help the buyers do their job for their own stores.

BUYER'S CLERICAL

For those with good clerical abilities, strong typing skills, a facility for working with figures, and of course, a fashion interest, the beginning job of buyer's clerical may be an excellent starting spot. This worker handles the many clerical records that supply the buyer with needed information. The buyer's clerical answers telephones, makes appointments for the buyer, follows up on shipments, and may handle problems related to late deliveries or damaged merchandise. The buyer's clerical has contact with the buyer and the assistant buyer as well. It is an on-the-job training position that can lead to advancement as an assistant buyer and eventually a buyer. Candidates for the position should be well organized, outgoing, be good with detail, have excellent clerical skills, and have the ability to work well with many different people. Buyer's clerical positions are usually available in both resident buying offices and central buying offices.

ASSISTANT BUYER TRAINEE

This entry-level position can be found in smaller resident buying offices or central buying offices. It is a middle-level job in large buying offices, but regardless of where it is offered, the position is a fine starting point for college graduates with specialized background in merchandising. Fast-paced, on-the-job training allows the assistant to help the buyer in as many ways as possible. Learning about major resources in any market usually happens when the assistant is assigned to do the follow-up tasks with the buyer. While working on-the-job, the assistant quickly learns to place special orders and reorders for the buyer. There is a heavy emphasis on keeping accurate records, following up on merchandise, and keeping in touch with manufacturers and stores.

At some point the assistant may go with the buyer to visit manufacturers and view merchandise. Later, the assistant may begin to handle a section of the market under the buyer's supervision.

In larger resident buying offices, each buyer has as least one assistant. However, in some smaller offices, several buyers may share the services of one assistant. The assistant buyer in a buying office tends to work fewer hours and fewer days than the assistant buyer in a retail store, and he or she often has fewer responsibilities. Therefore, salaries are lower. The skills needed to be a successful assistant buyer are the same as those required for the buyer's clerical, plus the ability to handle work under pressure and manage several tasks at the same time.

RESIDENT BUYERS

Resident buyers or market representatives spend most of their workday in the market. Before the store buyer arrives from out-of-town, the resident buyer searches the marketplace thoroughly for the latest items. The resident buyer offers ideas and information to the store buyer on the latest trends and the newest resources. He or she also may make suggestions about what the store buyer might consider ordering.

Once the store buyer returns home, the resident buyer continues to be helpful by placing orders and reorders. Part of the resident buyer's job is done in the office. Mail from the customer stores must be answered, manufacturer's salespeople who bring their lines in to be viewed must be met, and there is much telephone contact with out-of-town store buyers.

The resident buyer writes fashion news bulletins that are sent to all the member stores on a regular basis. These news flashes forecast the most current fashion information. With a particular client's approval, the resident buyer may even select additional items to be shipped to the out-of-town store. Basically, though, the three major tasks of the buyer are: researching the market, buying with the store's permission, and promoting the goods. The resident buyer's job is like acting as a consultant for people who need the latest fashion news. It is an ideal position for anyone with a keen interest in fashion.

The Central Buying Office

The central buying office represents its own chain of stores and has responsibility for centrally buying and selling goods in each of its stores. The individual stores do not participate in that part of the merchandising process. The buyer's clerical, as in the resident buying office, is often an entry-level spot in the central buying office.

DISTRIBUTOR/PLANNER TRAINEE

For those who have excellent math and analytical skills, are well-organized, and are good with details, the job of distributor/planner trainee may be of interest. Working with many precise records and computer printouts, the trainee keeps track of thousands of units of merchandise and assigns various items of stock to the many branch stores. A good memory and the ability to deal with many people, often by telephone or fax machine, is important for success. Promotion may be to head distributor/planner or to buyer.

CENTRAL BUYER

The central buyer is a specialist in the marketing end of buying for a large chain of stores or for a mail-order house. Central buyers work right in the major markets and buy for all of their stores. This means locating new and exciting sources of merchandise, making selections, and ordering and reordering based on what promises to sell well, be it for a few or a few hundred stores. The selling and publicizing of the merchandise and other related tasks are then left up to the individual store managers to handle in their own style.

THINKING OF YOUR OWN BUSINESS?

Why not? More and more men and women are becoming small store owners after obtaining some solid experience in the retail field. To be a succesful retailer, you must be a people person as so much of what is done involves the customer—how he or she thinks and feels about your products. A merchant must have a good sense of how to attractively and creatively display wares to help promote sales. You will need to rely upon good communication skills to deal effectively in the marketplace and then clearly convey current information back to workers in the store. You'll need to be able to function well under pressure, be a self-starter, and be able to do more than one task at a time without feeling stressed.

A thorough knowledge of all areas of retailing is an invaluable asset to any future store owner. At the start, small shop owners generally handle all aspects of the business themselves—choosing and buying merchandise from manufacturers or wholesalers, pricing the goods to be sold, having responsibility for the store's inventory, giving customers credit, collecting bills, and hiring and training a few employees. Selling the merchandise to customers may also be a part of the owner's task. This really means that the owner can become the merchandise manager, the buyer, the financial expert, personnel director, and public relations person all rolled into one. Chances are the owner of the store will be the housekeeper and janitor as well.

If the business thrives, the owner can then give some of these duties to other employees. Be prepared, however, for a lean period for the first few years, while the store is acquiring a reputation and a group of satisfied customers. Know, too, what all the financial obligations will be, and plan for their payment even when business is slow. Rent, electricity, advertising costs, income taxes, sales taxes, fire, theft, and liability insurance, and payroll costs all must be paid on time if you are to establish a solid reputation for your business. Generally speaking, retail businesses have a low survival rate. However, it is said that if a business can get through the first two years, the chances for survival are better—and the rewards are many. Certainly it's a great feeling to be your own boss and to decide where the shop will be located and what the image of the shop will be; and of course it's also a great feeling to succeed. Success rarely occurs by chance, however, and thus it is important for the small business owner to learn all there is to know about managing a business.

A growing number of small business owners are taking advantage of courses and workshops that have become increasingly available all across the country. Almost every business school and many specialized schools with programs in merchandising or retailing now offer courses relating to independent business ventures. Many adult and continuing education centers are picking up on this new trend too, and are starting to offer short seminars on small business operations. You can learn everything from how to raise venture capital for the new business to how to deal with the do's and don'ts of merchandising, from business law to financial practices. But before you even get that far, here's an extremely valuable bit of advice: Don't start your own operation without getting a good business background first!

If you are ready to work hard, the payoff of a career in retailing can be very gratifying and financially rewarding. One's earning power in retailing is impressive. It's a field that provides great opportunities and upward mobility faster than many other professions. As well, it's a good place for women and minorities to advance.

CHAPTER 5

CAREERS IN MANUFACTURING

The manufacturer makes it! This simple statement sums up the broad range of processes that go into the exciting path that fabrics and clothing take to get to the retailer—across our nation and all over the world. Because the showrooms and sales offices of clothing and accessories manufacturers, and even textile manufacturers, tend to cluster in fashion centers in certain parts of the country, you should consider exploring career opportunities in manufacturing only if you will be able to look for work in or near these geographic centers. Although it is possible to locate one or a few manufacturers in many areas in the United States, most entry-level jobs related to fashion merchandising with manufacturers are available in the well-established centers: New York City, Los Angeles, Chicago, Dallas, Miami, and Philadelphia.

And certainly the companies that manufacture fashion items are as varied as the items themselves. Consider, for example, the vast differences between the giant corporation that produces many kinds of clothing for children, men, and women, and the small company that makes only jewelry or gloves. Some operations are highly mechanized and quite sophisticated. Others still go by the hand processes used fifty years ago.

Jobs with manufacturers generally will be found in these areas: the promotion or selling of the merchandise, the merchandising or styling of the line, and the production and business end of the manufacturing process. For more information on the profitable and exciting possibilities open to sales trainees for apparel and accessories manufacturers, refer to the description in the chapter on the textile industry.

SHOWROOM SALES TRAINEE

An important activity takes place right in the manufacturer's showroom once a manufacturer's new line of goods is ready to be shown to the buyers who have arrived from all over the country. With flair and enthusiasm, showroom workers present and perhaps even model the new line of merchandise. This is the time for buyers to be told about the newest styling, fabric, or color that is part of the line. Here the trainee must learn to present the merchandise to buyers in the most appealing way. And if buyers place orders, the showroom trainee must write up the order neatly and accurately. It also may be necessary to deal with buyers on the telephone as well as in person.

Trainees follow up on shipments of merchandise, and may have some contact both with the salespeople who sell out of the showroom and the outside sales force in their various geographic territories. Answering telephones, acting as receptionist, scheduling appointments, and performing clerical duties all may be part of this assignment. Training is informal and occurs on the job. During busy periods such as *market week* when much of the buying for each season occurs, overtime work may be required.

Excellent grooming and appearance are needed for this diversified entry-level position with a manufacturer. Employers often specify a particular height or clothing size they would like candidates to be, if occasional modeling will be required. A friendly, outgoing person who is poised, confident, and speaks well will be an excellent prospect for this job. Employers generally request applicants who have completed a specialized program in fashion merchandising, though in some cases it may be possible to land this position without a degree. Once a trainee is completely familiar with the line, it is likely that he or she might be given responsibility for some smaller accounts. The next step could be advancing to showroom sales, merchandising, or piece goods buying.

SHOWROOM SALES

This inside sales position allows the showroom salesperson to present the line of goods to buyers. Showroom sales offers the opportunity to get to know active and important accounts well and to service their needs. Showroom salespeople also have the chance to act as the link between the design team and the buyers by passing on comments and ideas expressed during various showings. The salesperson also may be required to supervise showroom trainees.

Successful showroom salespeople who can communicate well, are good at the business of following through on customer service and production details, who dress and carry themselves fashionably, and who can present a line of merchandise at its best may advance to showroom managers. The showroom manager supervises all of the activity in the showroom and must keep the design staff informed of market trends and buyer feedback.

MERCHANDISING ASSISTANT

Working closely with the merchandiser, the assistant helps put the line of goods together for each season. The merchandising of a manufacturer's product is a varied and complex responsibility. Planning the line with the merchandiser requires some market research and an attempt to get to know what the customers want. The assistant needs to be familiar with the current market and with trends in colors, textures, fabrics, and new silhouettes. Other duties of the merchandising assistant include keeping neat and accurate records, filing swatches of fabrics, handling costing sheets, and helping to determine the price of each item. In addition, there is close contact with the merchandiser, the design and sales teams, the production staff, the piece goods department, and the buyers. Training is informal and is given on the job. During busy periods the assistant often is expected to work overtime.

Merchandising assistants must be well-organized, good at details, able to work under pressure, and capable of dealing well with many people. It is desirable to have a specialized degree in fashion merchandising for this position, which, depending on the potential of the employee, could lead to the positions of merchandiser or stylist.

MERCHANDISER

The merchandiser determines, based on the market research, the direction a manufacturer's line will take for each season. This information, along with an idea of production costs and data gathered in the field by the sales staff, allows the merchandiser to plan and promote the product. The merchandiser consults frequently with all available fashion resources and spends a great deal of time in the marketplace. These data are shared with the designer and perhaps with the owners of the firm before the overall look or direction of the line is agreed upon. In a large company, a merchandiser may be helped by one or more assistants. In a small firm, the designer or the stylist may perform this job.

Excellent knowledge of fashion resources, a keen fashion sense, and a knowledge of production processes are important for anyone interested in advancing to this position. It also would be desirable to have a degree in fashion merchandising or apparel production.

SHOPPER/STYLIST TRAINEE

These jobs are occasionally available with manufacturers, and often combine the varied duties of merchandising assistants, production people, and piece goods assistants. Under the supervision of a shopper/stylist, the trainee actively shops the market—retail stores and fabric houses, notions manufacturers, and trim sources—to help keep the firm completely up-to-date on the latest fashion happenings. This market research allows the shopper/stylist to gather enough information to be able to bring in ideas about style, fabric, and color that will be used to help create the next line.

Sketching ability is very helpful here, as the trainee must quickly sketch specific ideas that may provide direction. These openings are found in smaller firms that do not have a regular design room staff. In a large operation, a shopper/stylist trainee may be hired to assist the design staff if they are too busy to gather all the necessary information themselves. Qualifications and skills required for this position include an excellent fashion sense, a flair for color, and a knowledge of fabrics. A keen and observant eye for new trends also is essential. A portfolio of fashion sketches should be submitted to the potential employer when applying for this position. Employers are generally interested in hiring people with a fashion merchandising or textile background, though a fashion design background also might be helpful.

SHOPPER/STYLIST

The shopper/stylist has full responsibility for presenting new trends and ideas to the principals of the firm as well as to others involved in setting the look of each season's line. By sketching ideas and concepts on paper and thoroughly researching the fabric market, the shopper/stylist can put together a complete fashion picture for the firm. The shopper/stylist may work closely with the patternmaker and the merchandiser to help develop ideas. There is also an opportunity for fabric selection and coordination of the line. The shopper/stylist may be assisted by a trainee and then have the responsibility of training and directing that worker.

ASSISTANT PIECE GOODS/TRIMS BUYER

Piece goods are the fabrics the manufacturer uses to make garments. Trims are the parts of the garments you may not even notice—the zippers, buttons, snaps, or other decorations. Some trimmings are very noticeable, however. For example, the embroidered patches or appliques on your jeans or jacket may be the very reason you decided to buy them.

The assistant piece goods/trims buyer works very closely with the piece goods/trims buyer and assists by keeping clear and accurate records and swatch files; ordering fabrics, trims, and notions; and following up on these shipments and handling reorders when needed. Much learning occurs when the assistant goes with the buyer on visits to the fabric and trims markets. A broad knowledge of the piece goods business can be gained in this way. This job requires an interest in and knowledge of fabrics, an ability to work with figures and keep accurate records, and good communications skills. With diligent effort, this job prepares you for the position of piece goods/trims buyer. People with specialized training in either fashion merchandising or textiles will be of interest to employers.

PIECE GOODS/TRIMS BUYER

The piece goods/trims buyer has total responsibility for researching the textile and trims markets, and for buying these items. In larger firms, this position may involve the handling of many thousands of dollars worth of piece goods and trimmings each season. Piece goods buyers may work closely with the design and merchandising staffs to provide the latest information available about textiles and trims. In some cases, the designer makes all fabric selections for the piece goods buyer to purchase. In other companies, the piece goods buyers actually make the fabric and trimming selections from which the design staff works. If you have ever bought an item simply because you loved the fabric, you can see how important the job of the piece goods/trims buyer is.

IN THE "PERSONALITY BUSINESS"

By the time Sam was in junior high school, he knew he was heading for a career in fashion merchandising. A relative who was a buyer for a department store helped to make Sam aware of the fashion world. He knew more about merchandising than most of his friends. In high school, courses in distributive education gave him more information about careers and increased his interest even further. He chose a commercial curriculum so that he would be able to take more distributive education courses and learn more about this appealing field.

Through a part-time job with a local card and gift shop, Sam got experience in sales, stock, and window display. While still in high school, he applied for a sales job in the men's furnishings department of a large store. He was hired and loved working there. That experience convinced him seriously to consider the fashion merchandising field for his future.

Guidance counselors and teachers encouraged Sam to consider a college program in fashion merchandising and suggested the two-year degree in fashion buying and merchandising offered at FIT. Once enrolled in the program, Sam discovered he was in a comfortable setting where all the other students had the same interests and "spoke the same fashion language."

After his first year at college, Sam was one of eleven students selected for a special summer program at a large, fashion-oriented department store in New York City. Part of that summer assignment was a chance to work in the store's fashion office. Sam's task was to help stage a "Back to School" fashion show. This fabulous experience allowed Sam to work with buyers and manufacturers, help coordinate merchandise, and assist in window and interior displays. Once the program was completed, Sam and a few other students were asked to stay on to assist with a "Line for Line Fashion Show" put on at the Plaza Hotel in New York City. This added to Sam's unusual and well-rounded fashion experience that summer.

As part of Sam's school program, he was now ready to start his co-op or work-study assignment. He was hired at the department store where he originally had a part-time sales job when he was in high school. His position in the young men's department began just as men's fashions started catching the attention of the public. The department was very active, busily trying to keep pace with all of the apparel that young men were buying.

Two weeks after his co-op job began, the department's buyer became quite ill. Sam was quickly given the assistant buyer title and handled all of the Christmas business. It was a hectic time, but Sam took care of everything successfully. He was asked to stay on as a part-time department manager when the co-op assignment ended, and he did.

After finishing two active years at college, Sam was ready to enter the job market. With great enthusiasm, he accepted a position in an advertising agency working with several fashion accounts. It took him only two weeks to learn that the job was not right for him. Through FIT's placement office, he found another position as an assistant buyer for a catalog and discount chain operation. Working in the accessories area, Sam spent his time in the market, dealing with manufacturers of ladies' belts, hosiery, and costume jewelry. He learned a great deal about the workings of the buying office and gained experience analyzing the success of the items that were featured in the catalog for home shoppers.

Not entirely pleased with life in New York City, Sam took the bold step of relocating to Philadelphia. He sent his resume to every large retail store and had many interviews. Although he really needed a job, he was very clear about what he now wanted. His earlier retail experience convinced him that the men's wear area was the most appealing to him. And he wanted to be an assistant buyer.

When the store of his choice offered him a position, Sam was disappointed. It was a job in sales, as no assistant buying openings were available in the young men's department. Nevertheless, Sam wisely accepted the offer. He knew that with his flair and style, coupled with his experience and market background in New York City, he could be very valuable to the company.

Sam's personal manner of dress was helpful too. Sam quickly became a style setter for the department. The department buyer was happy to have such an aware salesperson and was receptive to Sam's ideas. He was soon offered the assistant buyer's job he wanted and worked at it for one year, bringing new life and vitality to that department.

The next step on the promotional ladder was an assignment as a group manager in a branch store. Store policy required this before Sam could become a full-fledged buyer. As a group manager, he learned a great deal. He supervised the entire sales staff, handled all customer problems and credit issues, supervised floor displays, and acquired broad administrative exposure. He was then asked to return to the main store, again as an assistant buyer, to wait for a buying position to open up.

During this waiting period, he involved himself with a new venture— handling fashion seminars for the branch stores. This was a chance for Sam to promote new looks and trends, and it was a great success. He coordinated an annual ten-day fund-raising event for a local hospital. He set up a small designer clothing shop for men and women, staffed it, stocked it, and chose all of the displays. He had full responsibility for this well-publicized and exciting event.

Still waiting for the buying spot to become available, Sam continued as an assistant buyer in the junior sportswear area for two years. He remembers this period with great delight. The junior sportswear department was bustling and very busy, and sold a complete range of fashionable items. He soon had the job of buying for one of the areas of the department, and business continued to grow. Sam received job offers from other retail stores during this time, but he held fast, indicating his loyalty to the store.

Finally, his patience paid off. A position as a buyer became available in the designer sportswear and accessories area. This was a new department in the store, and Sam truly wanted the job. He was interviewed by the store's merchandise manager and was offered the position. At age twenty-three Sam was a full-fledged buyer, and very proud. He knew that he was very young for so much responsibility, but he believed he was well-prepared for the job. It was exactly what he wanted.

A very elegant couture area was added to Sam's department, and that meant lots of travel back and forth to New York City on buying trips. After six months, Sam made his first buying trip to Europe. He returned enthusiastic and opened a French boutique in his department. It became a very successful operation, and still exists today, bringing glamour and style to the entire unit.

Sam's endless energy allowed him to put on twenty to twenty-five fashion shows yearly. He also ran an early morning fashion seminar, free to the public, covering various fashion topics. He worked with three branch stores coordinating and promoting their fashion merchandise. He developed good relationships with many of his customers and often bought for their individual requests. Active socially, he was able to get to know his customers at charity balls and fund-raising events.

Despite this exhilarating pace, Sam realized after a while that he wanted other kinds of retailing experiences. Sam knew he was ready for a change and began to consider other offers. A new and exciting prospect of coordinating men's wear fashions for an important department store chain in New York City was open. After several interviews with key executives in the firm, Sam was hired. He is in that position now, and has market responsibilities for men's designer and contemporary clothing and fashion coordinating responsibilities in all the men's furnishings areas.

In a newly established position with few set routines, Sam has the freedom to set up many of his own projects. After just three weeks at work, Sam was in South America developing contacts with manufacturers there. He continues to travel extensively, visiting manufacturers all over the world. He then returns to make slide presentations of what he has seen to the individual stores, so they are kept current and up-to-date. He researches new fibers, color trends, and styles and relays all this information to buyers before they go on their buying trips.

Sam's job is a very diversified and busy one. But he loves what he does. It taps right into his great style sense and flair for fashion. He believes he can work with many kinds of people and get them excited about new projects. Sam is now known in his field as someone who has a good record of accomplishments. He speaks of fashion merchandising as a "personality business," where cooperation and flexibility really count. He's active, energetic, and extremely dedicated to the dynamic world of merchandising.

CHAPTER 6

GETTING STARTED

It is essential for all job seekers to get to know themselves, as well as to learn as much as possible about various fields of work. This will help you begin to make the best possible choices in planning your career.

ALL ABOUT YOU

It's not easy to begin to know ourselves, and it's even more difficult to share that information with others. It often takes a lifetime to understand what motivates us individually. As we develop and change, our needs and interests change as well. Begin to pay attention to job-related interests that you can start to identify. Think about yourself as a "worker" and about the tasks you may be doing in the next forty years. Sound like a long time? That's often the amount of time a person spends at work during a lifetime. You should make this time an exciting adventure by gathering as much information about yourself and the fashion industry as you can.

It is indeed a discovery to start identifying real interests, skills, and abilities by taking stock of yourself. An inventory of what you like to do, what you can do well, and what you want to do in the future is the first step in the right direction. Matching your strong points with those required by certain careers will allow you to blend your best qualities with an employer's requirements and will provide for optimum job satisfaction. This process also can enable you to explore, as well as eliminate, job alternatives before you make your final choices.

ACCOMPLISHMENTS, SKILLS, AND INTERESTS

Think about your accomplishments. It may be difficult at the start, but it is an important part of helping you to understand your likes and dislikes, your skills, and the things that you value. It is helpful to put this inventory in writing. Take the time to think seriously about times that may have provided you with good learning experiences and include anything you feel you have done well in school, work, or leisure situations. For example:

Accomplishments and Activities

School	Passed tough math course in summer school
	Planned book sale to raise money for scholarship fund
Work	Held part-time babysitting job during first year of high school
	Salesperson at local department store during summer vacations
Leisure	My bowling team won first place in local competition last year

Now begin to take stock of the skills or abilities you used in each of the accomplishments you have listed. For each accomplishment, indicate the important skills used. For example:

Accomplishments	Skills or Abilities
	School
Passed tough math course in summer school	Ability to work with figures; problem-solving ability
Planned book sale to raise money for scholarship fund	Good organizational skills; ability to work with a large group of students, direct their activities and communicate clearly.

Work

Held part-time babysitting job during first year of high school	Ability to organize and plan my own time well; ability to relate well to young children
Salesperson at local department store during summer vacations	Learned to operate cash register; learned stocking and display techniques

Leisure

My bowling team won first place in local competition last year	Ability to work well in a team and successfully compete for a common goal.

Your particular likes and dislikes about your past activities can further aid you in identifying future career possibilities. For each item listed under Accomplishments, and Skills or Abilities, think about your likes and dislikes in the position. Jot these down in a third column, labeled Interests. These three areas, listed side by side, will give a composite picture of you as a working individual.

Accomplishments	Skills	Interests
	School	
Passed tough math course in summer school	Ability to work with figures; problem-solving ability	Liked challenge and sense of achievement in passing course
Planned book sale to raise money for scholarship fund	Good organizational skills; ability to work with a large group of students, direct their activities and communicate clearly.	Liked planning each student's assignment and meeting deadlines; disliked recordkeeping

Accomplishments	Skills	Interests
	Work	
Held part-time babysitting job during first year of high school	Ability to organize my own time well; ability to relate well to young children	Liked money and independent schedule; disliked travel to jobs
Salesperson at local department store during summer vacations	Learned to operate cash register; learned stocking and display techniques	Liked creating attractive displays; disliked dealing with the public
	Leisure	
My bowling team won first place in local competition last year	Ability to work well in a team and successfully compete for a common goal.	Liked competition

VALUES ASSESSMENT

The things and ideas you believe in are your values. They are often hard to identify, but they represent the various types of satisfaction you will get from your job, such as:

- variety of assignment
- adventure
- public contact
- working alone
- being creative
- job security
- travel
- status
- opportunity to learn
- nine-to-five schedule
- interesting co-workers
- advancement
- routine tasks
- urban setting
- high salary
- pressure
- risk/reward
- recognition

Choose five factors that are important to you and list them on a separate sheet of paper. Which segments of the fashion industry best correspond to your personal values? Patternmakers and retail fashion buyers, for example, often will have very different values and skills.

Now review your list of skills and interests and look for those that appear most often. As you have more and more experiences, your list of accomplishments and activities will grow. This gives you more information to work with in evaluating potential jobs.

Keep in mind the items you have identified as meaningful to you. As you learn more about various segments of the fashion industry, you also will discover a variety of job factors that accompany each position. It will be important for you to constantly re-evaluate these areas of importance as the information you collect about the fashion industry grows. You may change your ideas about what is important to you as a result of new information and more life experience. Look into all the career opportunities that seem to be in keeping with your educational goals, skills, interests, values, and life-style.

In addition to enabling you to make wise career choices, understanding yourself will allow you to present the best side of yourself to an employer. Unless you have real knowledge of your own strong points, it is difficult to convey your strengths to an employer. Concentrate on what you have to offer. Keep in mind that we all have limitations and areas of weakness. These weaker areas may change as you grow, and need not be viewed as permanent limitations. In fact, the ability to identify a weak spot may enable you to develop it, if you feel it is important for your overall career development. An earlier weak spot may turn out to be a selling point you can offer to an employer in years to come.

Now let's consider some simple tools that are essential for preparing for a job interview: the cover letter, resume, portfolio, and thank-you note.

THE COVER LETTER

The cover letter performs the task of convincing the reader (generally the employer or the interviewer) to review your enclosed resume and to consider you for an interview. It should be brief and to the point. The person reading your cover letter will learn of your interest in applying for a particular position and will hopefully be persuaded to read your resume for more details about you.

Each resume you mail to an employer should be sent with a neatly typed cover letter requesting an appointment for an interview. If you know who is responsible for hiring in a particular firm, check for the correct title and spelling of the name, and address your letter to that person. If you are not able to get this information, address your letter to the personnel director. Your letter should never exceed one typewritten page.

Sample Cover Letter

date

your current address
city, state, zip
telephone number

Ms. Amy Wong
title (Call the company and ask if you don't know it.)
company name
street address
city, state, zip

Dear Ms. Wong,

Professor Philips, my merchandising instructor, suggested that I write to you regarding the part-time sales position that is available in your organization.

As you will see from my enclosed resume, I have past sales and stock experience, and I am particularly interested in working for your store. I have heard of your excellent on-the-job training program and am eager to work and learn more about the exciting field of retailing while I complete my education.

I hope you will contact me as soon as possible so that we can arrange for an appointment to discuss my qualifications in detail.

Sincerely yours,

(your handwritten signature)
(your typed name)

THE RESUME

A thoughtfully planned and well-written resume may not get you a job, but it could succeed in getting you the all-important interview! The resume is a concise but complete outline of your education and work history, with some necessary personal details. It acquaints the reader with your goals, interests, qualifications, and experiences. It can be written in a very standard manner or in an individualized, imaginative style.

There are many ways of presenting information about yourself. As a beginner in industry, you will find that most employers or interviewers expect to have some written statement that describes you. In fact, many think of a resume as a means of "selling yourself" on paper. By carefully describing your accomplishments and highlighting your best points, you are creating an advertisement for yourself, which is an individualized picture of you for the reader. This can be a most helpful selling tool in your job-hunting campaign.

Don't underestimate the power of a neatly organized and perfectly typed resume. It can bring interest and attention to you and persuade the employer to grant you an interview. A well-designed resume is an "interview getter." Here are a few resume-writing tips:

- Make use of sample resumes and guide books, and be aware of different resume styles.
- Spend as much time as you need to clearly organize all your information.
- Revise your draft as many times as necessary until you are satisfied that you have covered all areas that may be important to share with the reader of your resume.
- Never misrepresent your experience or work history. Focus on your best features that are appropriate for the job. Be truthful and emphasize your strong points.
- Describe what you have accomplished, what abilities you have that will be of interest to the firm, and what you would like to be doing in the future.
- There is no need to include age, sex, marital status, race, or religion. You will be hired because of your qualifications, not because of these irrelevant factors.
- Do not type the word *resume* at the top of the page.
- As a beginner, your resume should not be longer than one typewritten page. It may be typed, or you may want to consider obtaining a good photo-offset copy of a typed original. Handwritten resumes are thought of as unprofessional. Messy resumes or those with typing, spelling, or factual errors are unacceptable.
- Always be sure to bring an extra copy of your resume to the interview.
- You can decide on the layout and spacing of your own resume. Be concerned with how appealing the information about you looks on paper. Remember—your resume is your advertisement for yourself!

Be sure that your resume covers the following areas adequately:

Name and Address. Your name, street address, city, state, zip code, and telephone number should appear at the center of the page or at the upper corner. It will identify the resume and indicate where an employer can contact you.

Goal. Always indicate your occupational goal and make sure it is in keeping with the job for which you are applying. It is never helpful to have a very broad goal such as "any entry job within the fashion world." Try to be more specific.

Education. List your most recent education first. It is not necessary for college graduates to list high school unless it was a specialized school. Indicate school name, dates of attendance, the degree received, and any school honors or scholarships. List courses or special programs that may relate to the job or industry. Include extracurricular activities such as clubs, student newspaper, or student government.

Work Experience. You may have some work experience as a result of summer and part-time employment. Briefly list it and describe your responsibilities and accomplishments. Be sure to list any industry-related exposure you may have had. As you gain professional work experience in the industry, you can then delete incidental jobs from your resume. List most recent jobs first and indicate duties you performed or promotions you received. Employers often are interested in knowing that students have held part-time jobs and maintained good school records, as well as appreciating the experience the jobs provided.

Unpaid Experience. Don't be modest about describing unpaid activities. Volunteer work is often very impressive to employers. This may include experiences in community groups, civic agencies, your church or synagogue, local hospitals, and so forth. Describe this area just as you would a paid position.

Special Skills and Interests. This part of the resume provides an opportunity to present interesting or unusual aptitudes and talents to the employer. Do you speak more than one language? Have you a unique hobby, are you a sports enthusiast, a skilled musician? A line or two about such abilities may be of interest to the reader and generally helps to present your personality in a more individualized way.

The easiest type of resume for a beginning job hunter to compose is referred to as a chronological resume. You begin by listing your most recent schooling and work experiences and continue to describe the rest in inverse order. It is easy to establish a simple outline of your experiences in this manner. Although beginners may not have extensive work records to refer to, keep in mind that employers are as interested in where you are going in the future as in what you have done in the past.

Sheila Mendes
125 East 8th Street
New York, New York 10003
(212) 555-2340

Occupational Goal	Assistant Store Manager
Education	Fashion Institute of Technology, State University of New York
Major:	Fashion Buying and Merchandising
Degree:	Bachelor of Science, June 1992

Major Courses	*Related Courses*
Fashion Marketing	Apparel Design
Consumer Motivation	Textile Science
Marketing Principles	Advanced Textiles
Fashion Buying and Merchandising	Fashion Art

Honors and Activities	Received Retailing Society Scholarship, Dean's list, Fall 1991, member of the Merchandising Society, vice-president of the Choral Society.
Work Experience *11/91–6/92*	Macy's Herald Square, New York. Work/study job in children's shoe department. Assisted customers, planned and designed displays, maintained stock inventory, sales increased by 25 percent.
6/90–8/90	Greensleves Camp, Copaque, New York. Planned and supervised activities for gifted children aged 8–12 years.
Special Skills	Fluent Spanish. Some travel throughout the United States. Can operate cash register and adding machine. Computer literate.
Interests	Member of the Arista Opera Society, guitarist, jogger.

THE PORTFOLIO

Although not all jobs in the fashion field require the candidate to present a portfolio to a prospective employer, most art and design-related jobs do. A portfolio should represent a collection of your best work and creative thinking put down on paper. An interviewer can quickly view your work and get a good idea of your drawing skills, sense of design, feeling for color and texture, and ability to coordinate fashions. From eight to twelve pieces of artwork should give any professional looking at your portfolio the opportunity to evaluate your strengths. It is not necessary to present all of your collected work, even though you may be tempted to do so. Beginners generally like to present all of their drawings, particularly early work, which is often amateurish. Employers are usually too busy to spend a great deal of their valuable time going over great numbers of drawings and designs.

What is necessary to achieve is a balanced representation of your abilities. If you are quite flexible in your skills, show samples of your work that will represent differing styles; let the viewer know that you can work in varied ways. For example, the textile designer who can draw in a bold, free manner as well as in a more detailed or tighter style, should choose several samples of each style of drawing for the portfolio. This easily demonstrates to the viewer that the artist is versatile and can do work in either manner.

Many employers discuss your portfolio with you during the interview to learn about your abilities, your style sense, and your ideas about fashion looks for the future. Other employers may look at your work but not discuss it with you at all. You should feel free to ask any viewer if they would like to have you talk about your artwork or your ideas. In addition to sketching, design, and color information, employers often can observe your creative thinking process by looking at your quick working sketches and then seeing your finished art work. It is interesting for them to note how the artist begins to put together a line or collection of coordinated fashions or fabrics. Be sure that only your most current ideas are shown during the interview. Employers do not enjoy seeing designs that are not truly up-to-date, and they are really most interested in discovering if your ideas are a season or two *ahead* of the times.

Employers naturally expect to see the very best artwork you can present to them. Neatness is critical! Messy, smudged sketches or poorly mounted work is a clue that you may be a sloppy worker. Clients will not accept less than perfect work, and employers consequently expect perfection from every artist they hire. So keep the following in mind:

- For many fashion jobs, a current and professional looking portfolio is required. Spend enough time on yours so that you can compete for the positions that do require one. Consult with and take advantage of the suggestions of your art teachers, placement counselors, and any working artists you know in assembling work that is suitable for you to show. It should reflect the most creative side of you to a prospective employer, demonstrating your design and creative abilities.
- Be aware of the kind of artwork each job opening requires, so that you can show an employer work that reflects what he or she may be seeking rather than unrelated items. What is suitable for one position may not be acceptable for the next job interview.
- It is not important to show your artwork in a fancy or expensive binder. Any folder that will protect your designs and help make a neat presentation is acceptable. All work should be the same size. Smaller designs can be mounted to be uniform with bigger pieces. Make sure each item of your artwork has your name on it for easy identification if you should lose or mislay it.
- It is not recommended that you leave your portfolio with an employer. If you are asked to do so, arrange to return at another time with your artwork, so that others in the firm may view it or so the employers can evaluate it for a second time.
- Never borrow designs from another artist and present them as your own work. You will be hired based on *your* creative abilities. Show only your own work in your portfolio.

GETTING READY FOR THE INTERVIEW

At this point, let's assume you've taken the necessary time to do your own personal inventory of your interests and your skills. You've prepared a thoughtful and letter-perfect resume and cover letter. If the jobs you are seeking require a portfolio, let's also assume that it is well put together and ready to be shown. The next step is preparing for the job interview.

The purpose of the all-important job interview is to allow the employer or the interviewer, as well as you, to make an informal decision about employment with a particular company. Employers can get a great deal of information about you from your resume, your portfolio, your image or style, the manner in which you respond to questions during the interview, and whatever else you can communicate in the twenty or thirty minutes spent in the interviewing session.

This is where advance planning can really work for you. Use the time you may have with each interviewer to communicate the best about yourself. It is your chance to convince the employer that you are really the best-qualified person to fill the job. Unfortunately, many job seekers do not do the proper homework necessary to present themselves in the best possible way for this important event. Consider the fact that a beginning job—gained as a result of a successful interview—may pave the way to an exciting and challenging career. Once you have specific information regarding an upcoming employment interview, try to keep the following in mind.

Time and Place. Be sure of the exact date, time, and place of the interview. If possible, get the name of the person who will interview you. Know how to pronounce the interviewer's name if it is a difficult one. Details concerning the interview should be written in a small notepad that you keep with you. Do not rely on your memory!

Allow enough time to travel to the interview so that you arrive ten to fifteen minutes earlier than your appointment time. Remember, traffic jams and other delays are unpredictable. Showing up late for an interview is never acceptable. Arriving a bit early gives you the opportunity to relax and to meet the interviewer in a more leisurely manner. Nothing is more upsetting than dashing into the interview, out of breath and out of sorts!

Research. Wherever possible, learn as much as you can about the firm. Talk to your placement counselor, teachers, or people you know who are working in the company. Very large firms may have annual reports or other descriptive material on file in your school or local library. If the firm you are researching manufactures a product, you can telephone the sales office and ask where the product is sold in your area. A trip to your local store can familiarize you with the manufacturer's price range and current line and give you an advantage over others who have no knowledge of the firm's product or service.

Take notes on the information you discover about each firm. You can review your notes before the interview and feel more knowledgeable when talking to the interviewer. This information also can provide you with material you may wish to discuss or question during the course of the interview.

Application Forms. Some companies, usually the larger ones that have a personnel or human resources department, will ask you to complete an employment application form. Be sure to bring a pen to the interview for this reason. Fill out the form as clearly and as neatly as possible. A messy or illegible application suggests that you are a messy and careless worker. Answer all questions so that the form is complete when you turn it in. If you cannot easily remember dates of part-time or summer jobs or other employment-related information, use your notepad to list all such details before the interview, and refer to it while completing the application form.

How You Look. Your appearance will be an important factor for all jobs in the fashion area. The clothes you choose to wear to the interview can give an employer an idea of your fashion sense and your level of taste. Although more casual clothing may be very acceptable once you are working, dress in a businesslike manner for the interview, and avoid extremes and faddish clothing or sunglasses.

Don't arrive with your arms filled with packages, bundles, or school-books. Leave all your gear outside with the receptionist, or better still, don't bring anything unnecessary along with you. Of course, never bring friends with you to an interivew. The first impression you make on the interviewer may be a lasting one!

DURING THE INTERVIEW

It is natural for you to feel nervous about the interviewing situation. You will find, however, that after you have had several interviews you do get some idea of what to expect. Certain basic questions almost always will be asked of you. You may begin to feel more at ease as you have more opportunities to practice your responses. As each interviewer operates in a different manner, it is best to be prepared for different possibilities by planning and practicing in advance. Think about answers you can give to commonly asked questions. Practice talking about your background, your goals and interests, your school preparation, and your ideas about your future. You can review this information about yourself with your placement counselor, with a friend or family member, or in the privacy of your room in front of a mirror. Interviewers often feel that the first few minutes of the interviewing session create the all-important impressions they are left with. With this idea in mind, be aware of your verbal presentation as well as your nonverbal presentation.

Your body language can convey a great deal! Good posture while standing, walking, or sitting is essential. Avoid slouching or slumping in a chair. Try not to fidget with jewelry, your hair, or your clothing. Do not chew gum. You should not smoke unless you are invited to do so. Increasing numbers of companies are asking that their employees not smoke, or that they smoke only in designated areas. If you know the interviewer's name, use it in an opening greeting. Try to maintain eye contact during the interview, although it may seem easier for you to avoid the glance of the person you are talking to. In an interview setting, avoiding eye contact can be interpreted as lack of interest in the situation.

Be honest in discussing your qualifications. Employers hiring beginners realize that you will not have a heavy work background. But let them know you are eager to work and learn. Remember to convey a friendly and positive attitude. This can help to put the interviewer as well as yourself at ease. Be natural and smile. Get information about the firm while you are giving information about yourself. Listen attentively, and express interest and enthusiasm while talking to the interviewer. If you sense the interview is going poorly and you probably will not be considered for the job, try not to let your disappointment show. Continue in a positive manner. Your confidence will leave the interviewer with a good impression.

Avoid taking notes during your interview. You can jot down any important information you may want to remember immediately after the interview on the notepad you keep with you.

Answer all questions completely instead of just replying with "no" or "yes" responses. Try not to wander off the topic or bring in unrelated or personal information. If you are stumped by a particularly tough question, let the interviewer know that you need more time to think about your response or that you are truly unable to to respond to that particular question. Once you are aware of a question you have difficulty with, you can prepare a better answer to that question in case it comes up in later interviews with other employers.

WHAT TO DO ABOUT SALARY

You will want to try to find out the salary offer or general salary range the employer is offering. You should be aware of what the minimum acceptable wage is for the beginning level jobs you are considering. Your placement counselor or teacher can be helpful in providing you with this information. Looking at classified ads in your local newspaper should give you a range for entry-level jobs.

If there is no mention of salary by the end of the interview and the job does appeal to you, you can feel free to ask the interviewer what salary the position will pay. Be prepared to be asked "How much do you think you are worth?" If you know the average range for the specific job, you can comfortably answer the question without asking for an unreasonable salary and without settling on a wage below the standard. Keep in mind that the salary should be discussed only if there is a real likelihood that you and the job are suited for each other. Questions about fringe benefits, vacation days, sick leave, and salary should not be asked until all other aspects of the job duties have been discussed and you believe you are a candidate for the position.

You should recognize that the starting salary is not the most important issue in deciding which position to accept. Find out the company's policy on salary review. You may take an entry job at a salary higher than one of your friends, but discover that you are locked into that salary for an entire year because your firm has a policy of an annual salary review. Your friend may have a chance to be considered for a raise in three or six months and may be earning more than you in a relatively short time. Unless you have great financial need, you should consider how much learning and training you can expect to receive and what promotional opportunities exist within the firm before making your final decision.

SAMPLE INTERVIEW QUESTIONS

Planning ahead for the interview is essential. Be prepared for some difficult questions. This is where your advance planning and preparation will pay off.

"Tell me about yourself" is a favorite ice breaker for many interviewers. You can start to talk about the items in your background that relate to the employer's job offer. Be specific and informative about your education, your career goals, and any work experience that relates to the work situation. This is your chance to display enthusiasm and to communicate your interest in the position and in the firm. Keep your replies focused on the job and its requirements so that you do not wander off onto unrelated conversation about yourself.

"Why are you interested in this company?" is another commonly asked question. Here is where your research will come in handy. If you have reviewed the firm's literature and all other resources, and in the case of retail stores if you have made a special visit, you should be able to discuss freely your particular interest in the company and what makes it appealing to you.

Become familiar with the questions that are most often asked during interviews:

- Tell me about yourself.
- What are your goals and career plans?
- Tell me about your strong points and your weaknesses.
- Why are you interested in working for my firm?
- How did you become interested in this field of work?
- What do you know about my company?
- What amount of money do you think your work is worth as a beginner?
- Tell me about your work experience while you were still in school.
- What jobs have you enjoyed the most? The least?
- What are your hobbies? Your interests?
- Discuss your school background.
- What special skills do you possess that will be important on this job?
- Can you take instructions and criticism without feeling upset?
- Can you work cooperatively with others?
- In what school activities did you participate?
- Did you receive any scholarships or awards?
- What courses did you like best? Least?
- What makes you think you will be successful in the field you have chosen?
- Do you like to work alone or with others?
- Do you have any questions that you would like to ask me?

Think about how you would answer each of these questions. It will help you to clarify your own ideas and to have answers ready at the time you need them. You should be prepared to ask the interviewer several questions as well, to convey your interest in both the job and the firm. Here are some sample questions to consider:

- How is the department organized?
- To whom will I report?
- Do people work in teams or individually?

- How often are there department meetings?
- Will I receive on-the-job training?
- Is the firm planning to expand?
- Are there new services or new products being considered?

You should know that it is illegal for an interviewer to ask questions relating to your marital status, age, race, or religion.

ILLEGAL INTERVIEW QUESTIONS

There are many federal and state laws that prohibit employers from asking questions about things that are not related to your ability to perform a job. Some of these issues include marital or family status, sexual preferences, religion, arrest record, national origin, and handicaps.

Because few supervisors or deparment heads are trained interviewers, many still ask improper questions, regardless of the industry or the size of the company. Most interviewers do not wish to ask illegal questions but during the interview may inadvertently lead the conversation into areas they should not be discussing. Your best strategy is to be aware of what questions you do not have to answer, or to practice how to effectively respond to such inquiries. In most cases, you can answer in a way that will allow you to retain your privacy without offending the interviewer.

Employers do have the right to inquire if you have a handicap that might affect your ability to perform your specific job. However, they cannot ask you to describe your medical condition to them. If you are questioned about a handicap, you might answer by saying that you are fully able to handle the responsibilities of the position. This type of response should address the interviewer's concern and allow you to clearly state that you can do the job.

CLOSING THE INTERVIEW

Assuming you and the interviewer have had a chance to talk and neither of you has any more questions, you can effectively use the remaining moments to try to leave the interviewer with a favorable impression by keeping the following strategies in mind:

Allow the Interviewer to End the Interview. Don't stand up or make motions indicating that you are ready to leave until your interviewer gives you the sense that he or she is ready to stand and terminate the meeting. At that point, of course you can rise and get ready to thank the interviewer for the opportunity of being seen.

Restate Your Interest in the Job. This is an excellent chance to once again talk about your enthusiasm and interest in the position, while thanking the interviewer for spending time with you. If you feel the position is an opportunity for you to make use of your skills and make a contribution to the organization, say so!

Talk about What Has Impressed You. Try to think about what part of the interview conversation impressed you. If you can remember items of particular interest, you should mention them. You might mention the firm's commitment to customer satisfaction, or the news that it is planning to expand or introduce a news product or service. The interviewer will appreciate that you listened attentively and have positive feelings about a particular aspect of the organization.

DECISIONS, DECISIONS

Following the initial interview, if you get an immediate job offer, and you are sure it is the job you want, accept it with a "thank you" and a definite "yes." Set the date and time that you will show up for work. Find out to whom you will report and know at what location you are expected. Make sure you are clear about the starting salary. Be prepared to fill out forms for the personnel and payroll departments. Call any other employers who may still be considering you and let them know you are no longer available. Show up for your first day on the job with energy and enthusiasm, ready and willing to work.

If you are doubtful about accepting a position that is offered to you, you can thank the employer for expressing interest in you and indicate that you need some time to think it over, or consult with your family or placement counselor. You can feel free to ask for any additional information that you may need to know about the company that will help you make your decision. Let the employer know exactly when you will call back with your answer and make a notation for yourself in your notepad. Be sure to contact the employer with your answer at the time and date agreed upon. If you decide to decline the job offer, express your appreciation for the employer's interest in you. Be gracious. You never know at what point in your career you may be very interested in considering employment with that firm again.

Employers like to know that you are interested in the job they are trying to fill. Convince the employer that you can do the work, that you want the chance to prove it, and that you appreciate the opportunity of having the interview. Relax, smile, and try to show as much confidence when you leave as when you entered the interviewer's office.

AFTER THE INTERVIEW

No interview is ever perfect. However, they do become easier with practice. After each interview, review the questions you were unable to answer easily and work on better ways to answer them. This will allow you to be more comfortable the next time that question is asked.

Keep your own record of which employers expect you to call back to hear about their hiring decision. Make a note of which interviewers plan on contacting you, and when. If an interviewer seemed interested and indicated that you would be contacted but you haven't heard after one week has passed, you can write a brief note or telephone to remind the interviewer of your conversation. Express appreciation for the time given you during the interview and indicate your continued interest in being considered for the job.

Don't become discouraged by a number of rejections and feel no one wants to hire you. You will learn a great deal from your early interviews and will probably do better in later ones. The job you are seeking may turn up when you least expect it. But you can't wait for exciting opportunities to come to you. Be active and pursue all leads that interest you. Follow them up in a businesslike manner. You must be aggressive and go after what you want!

THANK-YOU LETTER

A good way to improve your chance of making a positive impression is to send a letter of thanks to the interviewer. Take the extra time to write a short note of appreciation. Your thank-you note can be more than just a polite gesture; it can serve as a means of restating your interest in the position, and it allows you to summarize your skills and talents. In situations where your candidacy is borderline, a thank-you note may stack the odds in your favor. The same is true if you are competing with many other well-qualified candidates.

During the interview, you might think of asking for the interviewer's business card so you will be sure to have the correct name, title, and address. Write your letter as soon as you return from the interview and try to mail it promptly—no more than two or three days after your interview will ensure that you're still fresh in the recruiter's mind. A letter that arrives three or four weeks after the interview won't be of much value. After all, you want your note to have some impact on the hiring decision.

One or two well-worded paragraphs will allow you to express your interest in the job and your appreciation for the opportunity of meeting with the interviewer. You might want to briefly highlight your qualifications and indicate that you eagerly will be awaiting the company's decision. Try to make your letter personal by referring to some part of the interview conversation that you found interesting or helpful.

Your thank-you letter does not have to be typed unless you have poor handwriting. A neat handwritten note seems to get more attention as it feels more personal to the reader. Keep in mind that even a thank-you note is a sample of your work so don't get sloppy. Before you mail it, proofread it for accuracy, and make sure it's letter perfect.

YOUR FIRST POSITION

In fashion, as in any other field, your first position deserves a great deal of your energy and effort. Often, a first job will establish a pattern of achievement and advancement that will affect later jobs in a person's working life. It is a time to develop efficiency and organizational skills and to sort out future career options. A first position also affords the opportunity to improve interpersonal and communication skills. Properly selected and carried through, the first job can be an exciting and rewarding experience.

Here are some suggestions to maximize this crucial experience:

Be Prepared to Work Hard. Employers expect a full day's work from every employee. They often pay more attention to beginners, so it is likely that you will be observed more than experienced workers.

Be Observant. Try to take in as much as possible about all the operations you have contact with, not just those that form your particular responsibility. Being observant may allow you to pick up many valuable details about your work. Pay special attention to the way in which other employees handle their jobs; in this way you can learn the ropes more quickly. Employers will recognize and appreciate your interest.

Respect Your Co-workers. Experienced employees can be a wonderful source of information and advice. After all, who knows more about the unwritten practices of a company than a worker who has been on the job for many years? Use your co-workers as resources and respect their experience.

Find a Mentor. Seek out a senior worker who values your abilities and potential and who can give you new assignments, advice, and guidance that will help you progress. This personal relationship is especially important in larger, more impersonal companies.

Become a Do-er. Impress your supervisor with your energy and enthusiasm. You will soon get the reputation of someone who can be relied on to get a job done properly. This positive, active role will make your job more pleasant, and will count for a lot at promotion time.

Be Cooperative. Pitch in and help co-workers when you are able to without interrupting your own work schedule. You will then feel freer to ask them for help when you need it—and there will be many times when you will.

Mistakes Will Happen. Learn to acknowledge your errors and profit from them. No one demands perfection on the job all the time, and by admitting your mistakes you will quickly gain respect among your co-workers.

THE CHOICE IS ALL YOURS

Unfortunately, many persons find themselves in work situations that were never planned or even given much thought. This can result in years of frustration and unhappiness on the job. Remember the forty years of your working life mentioned at the outset of this book? Don't allow those thousands of hours of your life to be anything but the most rewarding for you.

The most satisfying careers don't always follow a straight path. Allow for detours as you move along. Consider exploring new areas of work—full-time positions, free-lance assignments, part-time jobs—in new fields. Determine how you can apply your skills and experience to new areas of endeavor. Look for the opportunity to get additional education.

Finally, leave time for your personal growth and development. Family involvement, travel, relaxation—all these activities can enhance and enrich your route to the top. Go for it. The choice is all yours!

CHAPTER 7

THE CANADIAN FASHION INDUSTRY

Canada's participation in the fashion world is as old as the country itself. Think of it starting four hundred years ago as French fishermen traded for beaver skins along the St. Lawrence River. These luxurious pelts were in great demand in Europe and inspired the exploration of other wilderness areas as far as the Pacific Ocean.

Today, Canada's supply of raw materials, as well as design and manufacturing talent, keeps her in the forefront of the international fashion scene. Canadian textile industries and clothing manufacturers are highly efficient as they face the challenge of these growing areas. Almost four thousand plants employ workers involved in the manufacature of clothing and textiles in Canada. The greatest concentration of these are found in Montreal, Toronto, Vancouver, Edmonton, and Calgary. More recently, smaller apparel centers have cropped up in Moose Jaw, Northbay, Cornwall, and Levis.

IN THE BEGINNING

The first kind of clothing for the settlers in New France and Acadia was rough and homemade. Historians tell us that the colonial and military officials had more luxurious choices as they imported clothing and furnishings from Europe. But clothes from faraway Europe not only were expensive but were ill fitting for the difficult life the settlers led. Every pioneer woman learned how to knit, spin, weave, and dye cloth for the entire family's needs for each season. They fashioned garments of homegrown wool from their sheep and coarse linen from their flax crop. A self-reliant breed, they not only produced their own fabric and apparel, but even built the necessary machines. Clothing was colorful, as they used the great supply of natural dyes from roots and berries, learned from the Indians.

THE 1800s—ORGANIZED MANUFACTURE BEGINS

The year 1820 saw the opening of the first woolen mill in Ontario and the start of the change from weaving and spinning at home. The manufacture of textiles quickly spread through Canada with wool and cotton mills springing up. Although Canadian homemade cloth was famous for its great strength and durability, factory production increased the demand for cheaper goods. Canadian flannels, tweeds, worsted, and cottons became sought after. In 1846, the invention of the sewing machine helped move home sewers, dressmakers, and tailors toward commercial production. An immigration drive brought millions of refugees to Canada. Highly skilled tailors from the workrooms of Europe became important in the manufacture of apparel. Men's and boys' clothing was first to be factory produced in Canada as early as 1868. These garments were cut from a paper pattern and then bundled together and sent to private homes to be sewn, with families paid for their piece work. As experienced seamstresses and tailors learned to fit clothing without working directly on customers, factory-made garments became more acceptable to the general public. By the 1900s, there were over fifty men's and boys' clothing factories and more thant two dozen firms manufacturing ready-made skirts, blouses, and cloaks for the ladies.

A NEW TREND

In 1902, a clothing designer from Montreal began a startling new trend! This designer introduced the first ladies' cloaks copied from those shown in New York City, rather than England or Germany. This marked the beginning of the influence of the established American fashion market on Canadian apparel. It was an era of simple, more functional design, as it moved from the elaborate style of the Victorian age to the industrial era.

The Canadian garment industry grew rapidly. Many skilled immigrant workers developed into trade union leaders and achieved vastly improved working conditions and wages for their co-workers. The development of standardized patterns after World War I helped the booming industry. It eliminated the tedious and time-consuming task of draping and cutting each new style, and it allowed for more efficient production at a time when the demand for ready-made clothing was on the rise. The styling and quality of mass-produced garments kept pace with the ongoing developments in the textile industry.

During World War II, the demand for fashion products coincided with shortages of both supplies and workers. Canadian designers and manufacturers were innovative in meeting the demand for clothing within wartime restrictions.

After the war, all areas of the Canadian fashion industry enjoyed a period of great prosperity and there was a need for men's, women's, and children's wear.

As the United States emerged from the war with new prestige, it offered competition to its neighbor across the border. However, the Canadian fashion industry promoted many imaginative activities and events to launch the best of the Canadian collections. Local designers and their lavish lines toured the country. The textile manufacturers organized the Canadian Association of Couturiers as a means of promoting high-quality Canadian fabrics. The Canadian fashion industry took on an agressive new image to meet the pressure of the American market and to deal with the flood of low-cost imports from the Orient.

SURVIVING IN THE 1990s

Apparel

The economic recession of the 1990s has affected Canada's apparel manufacturing sector, just as it has that of the United States. The president of the Canadian Apparel Manufacturers Institute (CAMI) believes that clothing manufacturers have been challenged by a growing number of obstacles and are moving quickly to respond. The effects of the downturn are reflected in goverment statistics that indicate that employment in the apparel manufacturing sector dropped almost 25,000 to approximately 100,000 workers in 1990. CAMI, the Ottawa-based association, believes that the industry is sufficiently able to overcome the hurdles and will start to see improvement!

The apparel industry must bear the burden of the Goods and Services Tax (GST), which went into effect on January 1, 1991. This 7% tax applies to most goods and services consumed in Canada. The customer resistance caused by these price increases may result in more cross-border shopping, sure to effect both manufacturers as well as retailers. To counter this, manufacturers are wisely using innovative marketing strategies. The United States remains Canada's major export destination through the 1990s, and extensive market research indicates that proximity to that market combined with great respect from American buyers for Canadian design and quality offers great potential to apparel manufacturers.

Encouraged by a greater potential customer base and the Canada-United States Free Trade Agreement, more Canadian manufacturers are doing business in the United States. Manufacturers who have been well established in the Canadian market are heading south of the border to open showrooms, start new divisions, and participate in trade shows. The number of Canadian manufacturing firms doing business in the United States is steadily growing. The Canada Apparel Center at the Canadian Consulate documents eighty apparel companies represented in New York City with about twenty-five of these firms in their own showrooms, representing women's apparel primarily but with children's wear and men's wear included.

Consider Peter Nygard, who has developed a Toronto-based moderate sportswear business and has built a bridge collection for the United States customer. His new line is sold to all forty-eight Saks Fifth Avenue stores throughout the country, with price ranges twice that of his Canadian collections.

Nygard believed this was an ideal time to enter the American market with a higher-price line because of the free-trade agreement between the United States and Canada. He has served as the chairperson of the clothing and fur sector for Canada's Sectoral Advisory Group on International Trade, which advised on the free-trade agreement. Effective since 1989, it allows tariffs to be phased out over a ten-year period. As a result his Canada-produced line, manufactured primarily in Winnipeg, is able to beat Hong Kong manufacturing rates.

The new breed of Canadian designers travels the world for ideas and inspiration, not necessarily relying on trends from Europe and America. Retail buyers in the United States, delighted with the design and quality of Canadian fashions and fabrics, include major Canadian fashion centers in their buying trips.

Fashion/Canada Inc., developed by the federal government, lends assistance to the development of professional and student designers who will strengthen Canada's fashion image. The group promotes Canadian designers both at home and abroad. The "Made in Canada" label offers high hopes for Canadian textiles and apparel!

Retailing

Promotional department stores are fast becoming the retail outlets of choice for Canadian shoppers. Lower-priced stores such as Zeller's, Kmart, Sears, and Woolworth, are managing to show solid gains in sales. As the majority of Canada's population lives close enough to the border to shop in the United States and return home in just a day, cross-border shopping remains a big issue for Canadian retailers. Over fifty-two million such trips were made by Canadian shoppers in 1990!

K mart Canada operates 125 stores and has plans to open another one. Donald A. Beaumont, CEO and president, states, "that the mass merchandisers are faring better than other retailers in this pinched economy." Apparently the tight economic situation has not bothered U.S.-based retailers who build more and more stores in Canada. New arrivals during the recent past include stores such as Toys "R" Us and the Gap, and club formats like Price Co., Costco, and Staples.

Textiles

A great deal of change has occurred since the textile industry's heyday in the earlier part of the twentieth century. Many of the smaller family-run firms have closed their doors or have been acquired by larger conglomerates. The shrinking of the textile industry is the effect of the advances in technology, research, and development that cause streamlining in every industry. The Canadian textile industry has had to adapt to this changing environment and is actively taking steps to ensure its strength. The well-organized Canadian Textile Institute (CTI) is working to see that the industry's needs are taken into careful consideration before decisions on tariffs and related issues are made at the federal government level. So there is great hope. With dynamic trade organizations looking out for the industry's best interests, textiles is entering another phase of development that should bring it with renewed vigor into the twenty-first century.

PROFESSIONAL ASSOCIATIONS

Here are the names and addresses of some fashion industry groups in both the United States and Canada that can supply you with more information on various aspects of the fashion business.

United States

Apparel Associations

Amalgamated Clothing Workers of
America
15 Union Square
New York, NY 10003

AMC Apparel Manufacturers
Association
1611 North Kent Street
Arlington, VA 22209

American Fur Industry
363 Seventh Avenue
New York, NY 10001

American Home Sewing Association
1375 Broadway
New York, NY 10018

Associated Corset and Brassiere
Manufacturers Inc.
475 Fifth Avenue
New York, NY 10016

Associated Fur Manufacturers, Inc.
101 West 30 Street
New York, NY 10001

California Fashion Creators
135 West 50th Street
New York, NY 10020

Clothing Manufacturers Association
(CMA)
1290 Avenue of the Americas
New York, NY 10020

Federation of Apparel Manufacturers
450 Seventh Avenue
New York, NY 10018

Infant's, Children's, & Girl's
Sportswear & Coat
Association, Inc.
475 Fifth Avenue
New York, NY 10018

International Ladies' Garment
Workers Union
1710 Broadway
New York, NY 10019

Men's Apparel Guild of California
(MAGIC)
300 South Grand Avenue
Los Angeles, CA 90071

Men's Fashion Association of
America (MFA)
240 Madison Avenue
New York, NY 10016

Men's Fashion Guild
47 West 34th Street
New York, NY 10001

National Association of Men's
Sportswear Buyers (NAMSB)
535 Fifth Avenue
New York, NY 10017

National Association of Milliners,
Dressmakers & Tailors
157 West 126th Street
New York, NY 10027

National Association of Women's &
Children's Apparel
147 West 33rd Street
New York, NY 10001

National Knitwear & Sportswear
Association (NKSA)
386 Park Avenue South
New York, NY 10016

National Outerwear & Sportswear
Association (NOSA)
240 Madison Avenue
New York, NY 10016

New York Coat & Suit Association
225 West 34th Street
New York, NY 10001

United Infant's & Children's Wear
Association
264 West 35th Street
New York, NY 10018

Western & English Manufacturers
Association (WAEMA)
789 Sherman Street
Denver, CO 80203

Textile Associations

Camel Hair & Cashmere Institute of
America
270 Congress Street
Boston, MA 02110

Knitted Textile Association
386 Park Avenue South
New York, NY 10016

Leather Industries of America
2501 M. Street NW
Washington, DC 20037

Man-Made Fiber Producers
Association
1150 17th Street NW
Washington, DC 20036

Northern Textile Association
211 Congress Street
Boston, MA 02116

Textile Distributors Association
45 West 36th Street
New York, NY 10018

Textile Salesman's Association
1500 Broadway
New York, NY 10036

Accessories/Jewelry Associations

American Footwear Industries
    Association
1611 North Kent Street
Arlington, VA 22209

Cultured Pearl Association
342 East 79th Street
New York, NY 10021

Diamond Information Center
1345 Avenue of the Americas
New York, NY 10105

Fashion Footwear Association of
    America
870 Seventh Avenue
New York, NY 10019

Headwear Institute of America
1 West 64th Street
New York, NY 10023

International Gold
900 Third Avenue
New York, NY 10022

Jewelers of America
1271 Avenue of the Americas
New York, NY 10020

Jewelry Industry Council
411 Fifth Avenue
New York, NY 10036

National Fashion Accessories
    Association
330 Fifth Avenue
New York, NY 10001

National Luggage Dealers
    Association
350 Fifth Avenue
New York, NY 10016

Retail Associations

American Management Association
135 West 50th Street
New York, NY 10019

Footwear Retailers of America
1420 K. Street NW
Washington, DC 20005

Menswear Retailers of America
    (MRA)
240 Madison Avenue
New York, NY 10016

National Mass Retail Institute
570 Seventh Avenue
New York, NY 10018

National Retail Merchants
    Association (NRMA)
100 West 31st Street
New York, NY 10001

National Shoe Retailers Association
9861 Broken Land Parkway
Columbia, MD 21046

Shoe Retailers League
275 Madison Avenue
New York, NY 10016

Councils/Bureaus

American Printed Fabrics Council
45 West 36th Street
New York, NY 10018

Color Association of the United
    States (CAUS)
343 Lexington Avenue
New York, NY 10016

Color Collective Council of
    American (CCCA)
175 Fifth Avenue
New York, NY 10010

Cotton Incorporated
1370 Avenue of the Americas
New York, NY 10010

Council of Fashion Designers of
    America
420 East 64th Street
New York, NY 10021

Crafted with Pride in the USA
1045 Avenue of the Americas
New York, NY 10020

Fur Information & Fashion Council
363 Seventh Avenue
New York, NY 10001

International Linen Promotion
    Commission
200 Lexington Avenue
New York, NY 10016

Polyester Fashion Council
415 Madison Avenue
New York, NY 10022

Wool Bureau Inc.
360 Lexington Avenue
New York, NY 10017

Women's Associations

American Women's Economic
    Development (AWED)
60 East 42nd Street
New York, NY 10165

National Association for Female
    Executives
1041 Third Avenue
New York, NY 10022

New York Women in Design
Network
180 Varick Street
New York, NY 10014

Women in Communications
415 Lexington Avenue
New York, NY 10017

Women's Sportswear Buyer's Club
1440 Broadway
New York, NY 10036

Miscellaneous

Costume Society of America
c/o The Costume Institute
Metropolitan Museum of Art
Fifth Avenue at 82nd Street
New York, NY 10028

Educational Foundation for the
Fashion Industry
227 West 27th Street
New York, NY 10001

The Fashion Group
9 Rockefeller Plaza
New York, NY 10019

The Fashion Society Design
150-10 79th Avenue
Kew Gardens, NY 11367

Fragrance Foundation of America
142 East 30th Street
New York, NY 10016

Millinery Institute of America
10 East 49th Street
New York, NY 10016

National Association Display
Industries
120 East 23rd Street
New York, NY 10011

National Home Fashions League
200 Lexington Avenue
New York, NY 10016

Public Relations Society of America
33 Irving Place
New York, NY 10003

Publicity Club of New York
60 East 42nd Street
New York, NY 10165

Society of Illustrators
128 East 63rd Street
New York, NY 10021

Underfashion Club Inc.
44 East 32nd Street
New York, NY 10016

Canada

Apparel Associations

Alberta Apparel Manufacturers
  Institute
  5240 Calgary Trail
  Edmonton, Alberta T6H 4W6

Alberta Fashion Market
  10403 172 Street, #300L
  Edmonton, Alberta T5S 1K9

Amalgamated Clothing & Textile
  Workers Union
  15 Gervais Drive, #601
  Don Mills, Ontario M3C 1Y8

Apparel Manufacturers Association
  of Ontario
  789 Don Mills Road, #700
  Don Mills, Ontario M3C 3L6

Apparel Manufacturers Institute of
  Quebec (AMIQ)
  555 Chabanel Street West, #801
  Montreal, Quebec H2N 2H8

Associated Clothing Manufacturers
  of the Province of Quebec Inc.
  (ACMPQ)
  555 Chabanel Street West, #801
  Montreal, Quebec H2N 2H8

Association of Millinery
  Manufacturers
  32950 Rene-Levesque West
  Montreal, Quebec H3B 1Z1

British Columbia Fashion & Needle
  Trades Association
  1100 Melville Street, #1330
  Vancouver, British Columbia
  V6E 4A6

Canadian Apparel Manufacturers
  Institute (CAMI)
  116 Albert Street, #803
  Ottawa, Ontario K1P 5G3

Canadian Association of Wholesale
  Sales Reps
  22 Leader Lane, #320A
  Toronto, Ontario M5E 1S5

Canadian Glove Manufacturers
  Association Ltd.
  PO Box 131, Station A
  Hamilton, Ontario, L8N 3A2

Canadian Ladies Fashion Institute
  444 Adelaide Street West, main
  floor
  Toronto, Ontario M5V 1S7

Canadian Shirt Manufacturers
  Association
  c/o John Forsythe Company
  536 Horner Avenue
  Toronto, Ontario N8Z 4X3

Canadian Sporting Goods
  Association
  1315 boul de Maisonneuve West,
  #702
  Montreal, Quebec H3G 1M4

Canadian Trimmings Manufacturers
  Association
  555 Chabanel Street West, #801
  Montreal, Quebec H2N 2H8

Canadiana Clothing, Textiles and
  Fabrics Association (CCFTA)
  5090 Explorer Drive, #510
  Mississauga, Ontario L4W 4T9

Children's Apparel Manufacturers
Association (CAMA)
8270 Mountain Sights, #101
Montreal, Quebec H4P 2B7

Fashion Council of Calgary
1106 4th Street SW
Calgary, Alberta T2R 0X6

Footwear & Leather Institute of
Canada
1010 Ste-Catherine Street West,
#712
Montreal, Quebec H3B 3R4

Fur Council of Canada
1435 St. Alexandre Street, #1270
Montreal, Quebec H3A 2G4

Garment Manufacturers Association
of Western Canada
435 Ellice Avenue
Winnipeg, Manitoba R3B I46

ILGWU—Canadian Office
9275 Clark, #200
Montreal, Quebec H2N 2K3

Lingerie and Loungewear
Manufacturers Association of
Canada
1435 Bleury Street, #600
Montreal, Quebec H3A 2H7

Manitoba Association of Designers
Inc.
484 Academy Road
Winnipeg, Manitoba R3N 0C8

Manitoba Fashion Institute
435 Ellice Avenue, #210
Winnipeg, Manitoba R3B 1Y6

Mens Clothing Manufacturers
Association Inc. (MCMA)
555 Chabanel Street West, #801
Montreal, Quebec H2N 2H8

Mens Clothing Manufacturers
Association of Ontario
789 Don Mills Road, #700
Don Mills, Ontario M3C 3L6

Montreal Clothing Contractors
Association Inc.
555 Chabanel Street West, #801
Montreal, Quebec H2N 2H8

Montreal Dress and Sportswear
Manufacturing Guild &
Montreal Manufacturing
Council
9250 Park Avenue
Montreal, Quebec H2N 1Z2

National Ski Industries Association
1822 Sherbrooke Street West
Montreal, Quebec H4H 1E4

Ontario Fashion Exhibitors Inc.
22 Leader Lane, #312
Toronto, Ontario M5E 1S5

Ontario Knitters Association
c/o Dorothea Knitting Mills Co.,
Ltd.
20 Research Road
Toronto, Ontario M4G 2G6

Prairie Apparel Mart
331 Smith Street
Winnipeg, Manitoba, R3B 2G9

Quebec Fashion Apparel
Manufacturers Guild
9250 Park Avenue, #300
Montreal, Quebec H2N 1Z2

Quebec Outerwear Knitters
Association Inc.
9200 Meilleur Street, 4th floor
Montreal, Quebec H2N 2B1

Rainwear & Sportswear
Manufacturers Association
555 Chabanel Street West, #801
Montreal, Quebec H2N 2H8

Shirt Manufacturers Guild
1080 rue Charette
Joliette, Quebec J6E 3P2

The Shoe Manufacturers
Association of Canada
4104 Sherbrooke Street West
Montreal, Quebec H3Z 1A8

Tanners Association of Canada
50 River Road
Toronto, Ontario M5A 3N9

Toronto Cloak Manufacturers
Association
444 Adelaide Street West, 2nd
floor
Toronto, Ontario M5V 1S7

Toronto Dress and Sportswear
Manufacturers Guild
444 Adelaide Street West, main
floor
Toronto, Ontario M5V 1S7

United Garment Workers of
America—Eastern Canada
500 King Street West, #230
Toronto, Ontario M5V 1L9

United Garment Workers of
America—Western Canada
331 Smith Street, #351
Winnipeg, Manitoba R3B 2G9

Western Apparel Market
910 Mainland Street, #28
Vancouver, British Columbia
B6V 1A9

Western Canada Children's Wear
Market
138 Portage Avenue East, #304
Winnipeg, Manitoba R3C 0A1

Textile Associations

Canadian Allied Textiles Trades
Association
49 Front Street
Toronto, Ontario M5E 1B3

Canadian Association of Textile
Colourists & Chemists—
Ontario section
47 Leslie Avenue
Cambridge, Ontario N1S 4N7

Canadian Bed, Bath & Linen
Association
31 Glenwood Avenue
Toronto, Ontario M6P 3C7

Canadian Textile & Chemical Union
40 1/2 Dalhousie Street
Brantford, Ontario N3T 2H8

Canadian Textiles Institute
280 Albert Street, #502
Ottawa, Ontario K1P 5G8

Cornwall & District Textile
Association
605 Boundary Road, PO
Box1328
Cornwall, Ontario K6H 5V4

Institute of Textile Science
1, rue Pacifique
Ste Anne de Bellevue, P.Q.
H9X IC5

Ottawa Valley Textile Association
334 John Street North
Arnprior, Ontario K7S 2P7

Textile Federation of Canada
1, rue Pacifique
Ste Anne de Bellevue, P.Q.
H9X IC5

Textile Society of Canada—Quebec
Division
c/o DuPont Canada
PO Box 660
Montreal, Quebec H3C 2V1

Textile Society of Canada—Western
Division
646 Alder Street West
Dunnville, Ontario N1A 1J5

United Textile Workers of
America—Canadian Office
4377 Notre-Dame West, #6
Montreal, Quebec H4C 1R9

Wool Bureau of Canada, Ltd.
33 Yonge Street, #820
Toronto, Ontario M5E 1G4

Retailing Associations

Retail Merchants Association of
Canada
1780 Birchmount Road
Scarborough, Ontario M1P 2HB

Retail Merchants Association of
Canada—Manitoba
2 Lumbard Place
Winnipeg, Manitoba R3B OX3

Retail Merchants Association of
Canada—Ontario and
Atlantic
1780 Birchmount Road
Scarborough, Ontario
M1P 2H8

Amalgamated Clothing & Textile Workers Union divisions:

Conseil conjoint de
Montreal—Division du
vêtement
20, boul de Maisonneuve
Montreal, Quebec H2X 1Z3

Conseil conjoint du
Quebec—Division du textile
440, rue Sud
Cowansville, Quebec J2K 2X7

Greater Cornwall Joint
Board—Textile Division
130 Sydney Street
Cornwall, Ontario K6H 3H2

Greater Toronto Joint Board
33 Cecil Street, #406
Toronto, Ontario M5T 1N1

Southwestern Ontario Joint
    Board—Textile Division
545 Main Street East
Hamilton, Ontario L8M 1H9

Toronto Joint Board—Apparel
    Division
33 Cecil Street
Toronto, Ontario M5T 1N1

Western Ontario Joint
    Board—Apparel Division
47 King Street West
Kitchener, Ontario N2G 1A2

Winnipeg Joint Council
138 Portage Avenue East, #505
Winnipeg, Manitoba R3C 0A1

EDUCATIONAL PROGRAMS

There are many different college programs available to you. Try to get as much information as you can about them. Each program is different and you should write to the director of admissions to request all the written material that is available for your field of interest. Wherever it is possible, try to arrange for a personal interview as well, before you make a decision about which school suits you best. It may be helpful to talk to teachers, students, and past graduates when you make campus visits. Be sure to ask about each school's connection with industry and the placement records of recent graduating classes. Note that some programs will offer a work-study experience that will give you an introduction and some practical exposure to an aspect of the industry. This may be very valuable to you and give you a glimpse of what goes on in the day-to-day activity in your area of interest.

Textile Programs/Fabric Styling Programs

University of Alabama, Tuscaloosa, Alabama 35486
> Residential environment in Tuscaloosa 56 miles southwest of Birmingham; coed; approximately 1,000 students; dormitory and dining hall facilities; scholarships are available; students admitted for fall, spring, and summer semesters.

College of Alameda, 555 Atlantic Avenue, Alameda, California 94501
Coed state supported college offering Associate of Arts degree; certificates offered for vocational majors; regional accreditation, Western Association.

University of Arizona, Tucson, Arizona 85721
Urban, residential environment; founded in 1891; coed; August, January, and summer semesters; approximately 4,000 scholarships available; all college sports offered.

Arizona State University, Tempe, Arizona 85281
Suburban environment east of Phoenix; coed; founded in 1885; regional accreditation, North Central Association; dormitory and dining hall facilities; $2 million scholarship fund for students.

Auburn University, Auburn, Alabama 36830
Small-town environment east of Montgomery; coed; new semester every quarter; regional accreditation, Southern Association; dormitory and dining hall facilities; housing available in private homes and apartments; some fellowships and scholarships available.

Barat College, Lake Forest, Illinois 60045
Located in a Chicago suburb; a Catholic-related college for 850 women offering a strong liberal arts program. Specially trained faculty advisors assist each student in developing an individually planned program offering study abroad, off-campus internships, and independent research; residence hall and dining hall facilities; many scholarships available.

Boston University, Commonwealth Avenue, Boston, Massachusetts 02215
Urban environment along the Charles River; coed; students admitted in September term; dormitory and dining hall facilities; freshman scholarships exceed $2 million; limited number of scholarships are available to academically gifted students based on their scholastic record; all college sports offered.

Brevard College, Brevard, North Carolina 28712
Located in the heart of the Blue Ridge Mountains; coed; two-year programs; semesters begin August and January; dormitory and dining hall facilities; financial aid available on basis of ability, character, and need; accredited by Southern Association.

Brigham Young University, Provo, Utah 84601
>Small-city environment 40 miles southeast of Salt Lake City; coed; private institution founded in 1875; full-time day and evening school; dormitory and dining hall facilities; 2,500 undergraduate scholarships are granted.

University of California, Davis, California 95616
>Rural environment, 13 miles west of Sacramento; coed; students admitted January, March, and September; regional accreditation, Western Association; no tuition for California state residents; undergraduate scholarships available.

California College of Arts and Crafts, Oakland, California 94618
>Urban environment; coed; full- and part-time degree and nondegree programs offered; classes begin January, May, June, July, September; regional accreditation, Western Association; residence halls for women only; coed residence halls available in the summer; 3-year certificate programs and 4-year degree programs offered.

Center for Creative Studies, College of Art and Design, Detroit, Michigan 48202
>Formerly known as Art School of the Society of Arts and Crafts; regional accreditation, North Central Association.

Chamberlayne Jr. College, 128 Commonwealth Avenue, Boston, Massachusetts 02116
>Urban environment; coed; private institution founded 1892; 2-year programs offering associate degrees, dormitory and dining halls available.

Colorado State University, Fort Collins, Colorado 80523
>Small-city environment 65 miles north of Denver; coed; state-supported institution founded in 1870; residence halls available; scholarships mainly for Colorado state residents; part-time jobs available for qualified students.

Delta College, University Center, Michigan 48710
>Coed; publicly-controlled institution founded in 1957; full- and part-time programs; dormitory facilities; 2-year degree programs offered; regional accreditation, North Central Association.

Edinboro State College, Edinboro, Pennsylvania 16444
>Small-town environment 18 miles south of Erie; coed; state-controlled institution founded in 1857; full-time and part-time programs; dormitory

and dining hall facilities; financial aid and part-time jobs available; all college sports offered.

Fashion Institute of Technology, 227 West 27th Street, New York, New York 10001

Coed; special college under the program of the State University of New York sponsored by the Board of Education of the City of New York; 1-, 2-, 4-year and Master's Degree programs available; students admitted September, February; dormitory and dining hall facilities; financial aid and scholarship programs available, many industry related; full-time and part-time programs during the day, evenings, and weekends; regional accreditation, Middle States Association.

Illinois State University, Normal, Illinois 61761

Small-city environment; coed; state university founded in 1857; first-year students enter in August, January, June; regional accreditation, North Central Association; dormitory and dining hall facilities; part-time jobs and some special awards are available; all college sports offered.

Indiana University, Bloomington, Indiana 47401

Small-city environment 52 miles southwest of Indianapolis; coed; state university founded in 1820; regional accreditation, North Central Association; dormitory and dining hall facilities; many students earn all or part of the tuition as a result of liberal financial aid plans; all college sports offered.

University of Iowa, Iowa City, Iowa 52242

Small-town environment; coed; state institution founded in 1847; regional accreditation, North Central Association; dormitory and dining halls available; 1,000 scholarships.

University of Kansas, Lawrence, Kansas 66044

City environment; coed; state university founded in 1866; regional accreditation, North Central Association; dormitory and dining hall facilities; 2,500 scholarships and fellowships available.

University of Kentucky, Lexington, Kentucky 40506

Urban environment; coed; state university founded in 1865; first-year students admitted fall, spring, or summer quarter; financial aid program includes grants, loans, scholarships, and work-study programs.

Louisville School of Art, 100 Park Road, Anchorage, Kentucky 40223
Rural environment 13 miles east of Louisville; coed; private college of fine arts founded in 1929; portfolio of applicant's art work required with other admissions materials; no housing on campus; federal financial aid program.

Mankato State University, Mankato, Minnesota 56001
Small-city environment 75 miles southwest of Minneapolis; coed; state institution founded in 1868; full-time and part-time programs; students admitted September, January, March, June, July; dormitory and dining hall facilities; financial aid program plus scholarships available.

Marywood College, Scranton, Pennsylvania 18509
Suburban, residential environment; liberal arts college for women founded in 1915; first-year students admitted September; scholarships and financial aid program available.

Massachusetts College of Art, Boston, Massachusetts 02215
Urban environment; coed; state-controlled institution; first-year students admitted September; no dormitory facilities.

Mercyhurst College, Erie, Pennsylvania 16501
Suburban, residential environment; coed; liberal arts Christian college with a Catholic heritage; first-year students admitted September, January, March; dormitory and dining hall facilities; honor and athletic scholarships available; financial aid programs and student service programs.

Michigan State University, East Lansing, Michigan 48824
Residential community near the state capitol; coed; state-controlled institution founded in 1855; many foreign students; students admitted January, March, June, September; dormitory and dining hall facilities; numerous scholarships and financial aid programs; all college sports offered.

University of Minnesota, Minneapolis, Minnesota 55455
Coed; state supported land-grant institution founded in 1851; dormitory and dining halls available plus housing for students with local families; 500 undergraduate scholarships and financial aid available.

Moorhead State University, Moorhead, Minnesota 56560
Small-city environment in the western part of Minnesota; near Fargo, North Dakota; coed; state college founded in 1887; students admitted September, January, March, June, July; dormitories and food service available; 65 scholarships and financial aid programs; 2- and 4-year programs offered.

University of Nebraska, Lincoln, Nebraska 68508
Urban environment; coed; state-controlled land-grant institution founded in 1871; sessions begin August, January, June, July; dormitory and dining hall facilities; 1,200 scholarships and fellowships available; competitive scholarships for Nebraska high school graduates; financial aid program.

North Carolina State University, Raleigh, North Carolina 27650
Urban environment; coed; land-grant school founded in 1887; dormitory facilities; dining halls operate on the cafeteria system; financial aid awards based on need and academic promise; work-study programs offered.

Northeastern Oklahoma State University, Tahlequah, Oklahoma 74464
Small-town, rural environment; northeast of Muskogee; coed; state-controlled school founded in 1846 by the Cherokee Indian Nation.

Northern Michigan University, Marquette, Michigan 49855
Small-city environment on the south shore of Lake Superior; coed; state-controlled school founded in 1899; students admitted August, December, April, May; residence hall facilities; 1,500 scholarship awards for academic achievement; college sports offered.

Ohio State University, Columbus, Ohio 43210
Urban environment; coed; state assisted land-grant school founded in 1870; dormitory facilities; Ohio Instructional Grants available to low income Ohio residents; approximately 5,000 part-time jobs available on-campus; financial aid program.

Philadelphia College of Textiles and Science, School House Lane, Germantown, Philadelphia, Pennsylvania 19144
America's oldest textile college in a suburban environment; coed; founded in 1884; residence halls plus housing available in private homes with local families; cafeteria facility; all sports offered; many scholarships from

industry; other scholarships awarded on need and scholastic achievement; financial aid programs,

Radford College, Radford, Virginia 24142

Small-city environment, 40 miles southwest of Roanoke; coed; founded in 1913; dormitory and dining hall facilities; scholarships and loan funds available.

Rochester Institute of Technology, Rochester, New York 14623

New suburban campus built in 1968; coed; private technological institution founded in 1829; day and evening programs; residence hall facilities; first-year students admitted September; scholarships available, some industry sponsored; work-study programs; college sports offered; 2- and 4-year programs.

Rosary College, River Forest, Illinois 60305

Suburban environment, 10 miles west of Chicago; coed; operated by Dominican Sisters of Sinsinawa, Wisconsin; founded in 1901; September and mid-year admissions; dormitory and dining hall facilities; approximately 140 freshman scholarships, awards, and loan funds, federal financial aid programs available.

Seattle Pacific University, Seattle, Washington 98119

Urban, residential environment coed; arts and science college with specialized curricula, private; sponsored by Free Methodist Church; founded in 1891; residence halls, boarding facilities; student work program; some college sports offered; scholarships available.

Skidmore College, Saratoga Springs, New York 12866

Small resort city with cultural environment; 32 miles north of Albany; coed; private college founded in 1911; first-year students admitted September, February; residence halls and dining hall facilities, student townhouse apartments; comprehensive financial aid program (scholarships, grants, loans, campus employment) to assist all who qualify with demonstrated need; full sports offered.

South Dakota State University, Brookings, South Dakota 57007

Rural environment north of Sioux Falls; coed; state-controlled university founded in 1884; students admitted August, January; dormitory and dining hall facilities; loan fund available.

Southern Illinois University, Carbondale, Illinois 62901
Small-city environment; coed; state university founded in 1869; fall, spring, summer terms; 2- and 4-year programs; university housing facilities; financial aid and campus employment offered.

Southwest Missouri State University, Springfield, Missouri 65802
Urban environment; coed; state university; students admitted August, January, June; residence hall facilities.

St. Philip's College, San Antonio, Texas 78203
Coed; publicly-controlled college; living facilities available.

St. Vincent College, Latrobe, Pennsylvania 15650
Small-city environment 40 miles east of Pittsburgh; men's private college; exchange program with Seton Hill Women's College; founded in 1846; full financial aid programs available; college sports offered.

Syracuse University, Syracuse, New York 13210
Urban environment; coed; privately controlled; founded in 1870 by the Methodist Church with financial support from the City of Syracuse; dormitory and dining hall facilities; wide variety of financial aid programs; undergraduates awarded scholarships, grants loans, and campus employment opportunities.

University of Tennessee, Knoxville, Tennessee 37916
Urban environment, state-controlled coed institution; founded in 1794; dormitory and cafeteria facilities; 500 scholarships available; loan fund.

Utah State University, Logan, Utah 84321
Small-city environment; coed; state-controlled; founded in 1890; first-year students admitted each quarter; dormitory, residence halls, and dining hall facilities; scholarship and loan funds available; college sports offered.

Ventura College, Ventura, California 93003
Coed; operated by Ventura County Jr. College District; 13th and 14th grades of liberal arts and preprofessional programs; day and evening programs; A.A. degree awarded.

University of Vermont, Burlington, Vermont 05401
Urban environment; coed; state-controlled institution; founded in 1791; receives state and federal funds; financial aid awarded on basis of financial need; residence halls, dining hall, and cafeteria facilities.

Virginia Commonwealth University, 910 West Franklin Street, Richmond, Virginia 23284

Founded in 1838; first-year students enter September, January; residence hall facilities; financial aid and loan fund programs; college sports offered.

Virginia State College, Petersburg, Virginia 23802

Suburban environment; coed; state-controlled land-grant college; founded in 1882; dormitory facilities; financial aid, scholarships, loans, grants, and student employment offered.

Wayne State University, Detroit, Michigan 48202

Urban environment; coed; state-controlled; first-year students admitted September, January, April, summer session; dormitory and apartment facilities; 3,800 scholarships generally limited to Michigan state residents; loan fund available.

Western Michigan University, Kalamazoo, Michigan 49001

Urban environment; coed; state-controlled institution founded in 1903; students admitted August, January, April, June to full-time and part-time programs; dormitory and dining hall facilities; 1,500 scholarships and financial programs available.

University of Wisconsin, Madison, Wisconsin 53706

Urban environment, lakeshore city; coed; founded in 1942; first-year students admitted fall, winter, summer; dormitory and dining hall facilities; scholarships and substantial loan and student employment programs available, including work-study program.

University of Wisconsin, Stevens Point, Wisconsin 54481

Located in urban area; coed; state-supported institution founded in 1894; first-year students admitted all semesters and summer; residence halls and dormitory facilities; federal financial assistance plus loans, work programs, and scholarships available.

Apparel Design, Fashion Merchandising, and Manufacturing Management

University of Akron, Akron, Ohio 44325

Urban environment; coed; state university founded in 1870 by the Universalist Church; became part of the State University in 1967; first-year students admitted any semester; dormitory and dining hall facilities; 1,250 scholarships available as well as loan fund and federal financial aid programs.

University of Alabama—see Textile Programs

College of Alameda—see Textile Programs

Albion College, Albion, Michigan 49224
Small-city environment 90 miles west of Detroit; privately controlled; related to the United Methodist Church; founded in 1835; dormitory and dining hall facilities; student employment, loans, scholarships available.

Aquinas College, Grand Rapids, Michigan 49506
Urban environment; coed; Roman Catholic institution founded in 1886; became a junior college in 1931; first-year students admitted August, January; dormitory facilities; scholarship and loan fund available; college sports offered.

University of Arizona—see Textile Programs

Art Institute of Chicago, Michigan Avenue at Adams Street, Chicago, Illinois 60603
Urban, downtown environment; coed; school of fine arts and design; privately operated as a non-profit division of the semipublic museum, Art Institute, founded in 1866; no dormitory facilities or athletic programs; financial aid available.

Auburn University—see Textile Programs

Bauder College, 1321 Howe Avenue, Sacramento, California 95825
Women's private college offering 2-year A.A. degree programs; apartments available.

Bauder Fashion College, 100 S.E. Fourth Street, Miami, Florida 33131
Coed; private; offers 2-year A.A. degree program in fashion design; 1-year program leads to fashion merchandise diploma; internships available.

Bay Path Jr. College, Longmeadow, Massachusetts 01106
Suburban environment, beautiful campus set in historic New England community near Springfield; private; 2-year college for women founded in 1897; offers Associate in arts and associate in science degree programs.

Becker Jr. College, 61 Sever Street, Worcester, Massachusetts 01609
   Coed; private college founded in 1887; A.S. degree programs; career
   internship and co-op education available in all programs.

Benedictine College, Atchison, Kansas 66002
   Small-city environment 45 miles northwest of Kansas City; coed;
   sponsored by Benedictines; dormitory and dining facilities; complete
   financial aid programs; academic, athletic, and leadership scholarships
   awarded on a no-need basis.

*Bethany Lutheran College, 734 Marsh Street, Mankato, Minnesota
56001*
   Coed; private, residential junior college supported by the Evangelical
   Lutheran Synod; pre-professional curricula combined with Christian
   course offerings; A.A. degree offered; financial aid available.

Bethany Nazarene College, Bethany, Oklahoma 73008
   Small-town suburban environment 10 miles northwest of the center of
   Oklahoma City; coed; private school operated by the Church of the
   Nazarene; dormitory, dining hall, and cafeteria facilities; honor
   scholarships for outstanding students available; loan fund and 25 alumni
   foundation scholarships; college sports offered.

*Brevard Community College, 1519 Clearlake Road, Cocoa, Florida
32922*
   Coed; publicly controlled; operated by the state of Florida; no dormitory;
   modern dining facility; A.A. and A.S. degree programs offered.

Brigham Young University—see Textile Programs

*County of Broward Community College, 225 E. Las Olas Boulevard,
Fort Lauderdale, Florida 33301*
   Coed; under the supervision of the State Department of Education; no
   dormitory or dining hall facilities; A.A., A.A.S., and A.S. degree
   programs; vocational courses also are offered.

*California State University, Shaw and Cedar Avenues, Fresno,
California 93740*
   Suburban campus; coed; founded in 1910 as the first junior college in
   California; offers 2- and 4-year programs; residence hall and cafeteria
   facilities; full financial aid programs available.

Cazenovia College, Cazenovia, New York 13035
  Women's private independent institution founded in 1824; financial aid
  program available; A.A., A.A.S., and A.S. degrees offered as well as
  1-year certificate programs.

Cheyney State College, Cheyney, Pennsylvania 19319
  Suburban area 25 miles northwest of Philadelphia; coed; one of 14
  state-owned Pennsylvania colleges; founded in 1837 and the oldest public
  college in the United States founded for black students; grants, loans, and
  student employment available.

*Chicago Academy of Fine Arts, 65 E. South Water Street, Chicago,
  Illinois 60601*
  Urban environment; coed; privately controlled institution; students
  admitted September, February, June; nine-month day school programs
  offered leading to certificates, diplomas, and associate or B.F.A. degrees.

University of Cincinnati, Cincinnati, Ohio 45221
  Urban environment; coed institution founded in 1891; first-year students
  admitted fall, winter, summer quarters; dormitory and dining hall
  facilities; scholarships and loan funds available, including industry
  scholarships; was the first institution in the United States to adopt a co-op
  plan, (1906) alternating work and study.

Clark College, Atlanta Georgia 30314
  Urban; coed; privately controlled college cooperating with the Atlanta
  University Center; founded in 1869; dormitory and dining hall facilities;
  scholarships and grants include work awards; loan fund.

Coffeyville Community Jr. College, Coffeyville, Kansas 67737
  Coed; operated by the county district for the 13th and 14th grades;
  dormitory facilities; day and evening programs leading to A.A. degree;
  Federal financial aid; co-op work-study programs available.

Columbia College, Eighth and Rogers, Columbia, Missouri 65201
  Private, independent college offering 2- and 4-year programs coordinated
  with the University of Missouri; coed; students admitted August, January;
  dormitory and dining hall facilities.

Columbia Commercial College, 1234 Hampton, Columbia, South Carolina 29201
> Coed; 2-year institution offering associate degree; apartment facilities; financial aid available.

University of Connecticut, Storrs, Connecticut 06268
> Rural environment; coed; state university founded in 1881; students admitted September, January; dormitory and dining hall facilities; more than 400 scholarships and fellowships available.

Delta College—see Textile Programs

College of the Desert, 43-500 Monterey Avenue, Palm Desert, California 92260
> Coed; terminal and transfer programs offered; tuition free to California residents; off-campus dormitory facilities; associate degree programs.

Drexel University, Philadelphia, Pennsylvania 19104
> Urban environment, coed; private, professional and technical institution; approximately 6,000 students; endowments and scholarships available; a majority of the students earn a portion of their expenses on co-op education plan; dormitory facilities.

College of DuPage, 22nd Street and Lambert Roads, Glen Ellyn, Illinois 60137
> Coed; junior college founded in 1966; about 19,000 students; students admitted throughout the year if they are high school graduates or 18 years of age; transfer and terminal programs leading to associate degree; no dormitory facilities.

Eastern Illinois University, Charleston, Illinois 61920
> Small-city environment 175 miles south of Chicago; coed; residence halls and food service facilities; scholarships available.

Eastern Michigan University, Ypsilanti, Michigan 48197
> Small-city environment between Detroit and Ann Arbor; coed; over 1,000 university scholarships ranging from $50 to $1,250; college work-study, grants, loans available.

El Paso Community College, 432 Frederick, El Paso, Texas 79915
> Coed; open door admissions policy; no on-campus housing; $100 per semester; associate degree awarded.

Fashion Institute of Technology—see Textile Programs

Florida A. & M. University, Tallahassee, Florida 32307
Urban environment; coed; state-supported institution; dormitory facilities; associate, baccalaureate, and graduate degrees conferred.

Fullerton College, Fullerton, California 92634
Coed; associate, baccalaureate, and graduate degrees.

George C. Wallace State Community College, Dothan, Alabama 36301
Coed; public institution; no dormitory facilities; open admissions with high school transcript or the equivalent; Associate in Arts or Science degrees awarded.

University of Georgia, Athens, Georgia 30601
Urban environment; coed; state supported; dormitory facilities; 350 to 400 scholarships and loans available.

Georgia Southern College, Statesboro, Georgia 30458
Small-town environment near Savannah; state-supported institution founded in 1906; dormitory facilities; work-study, scholarships, and loan fund available; intercollegiate athletics offered.

Grand Rapids Jr. College, Grand Rapids, Michigan 49502
Coed; publicly controlled institution; first-year students admitted on high school graduation; supervised housing and dining hall facilities; A.S. and A.A.S. degrees awarded.

Green Mountain College, Poultney, Vermont 05764
Located in the heart of Vermont's recreational and skiing areas; 155-acre campus; coed; private 2- and 4-year college.

Harcum Jr. College, Bryn Mawr, Pennsylvania 19010
Independent, nonprofit women's college founded in 1915; 2-year transfer or career curricula leading to A.A. and A.S. degrees.

University of Hawaii, Honolulu, Hawaii 96822
Urban residential environment; supported by state and federal governments; coed; admission dependent upon performance on college aptitude tests, quality of high school work, and various ratings by

preparatory school; limited dormitory facilities; most scholarships restricted to state residents; intercollegiate athletics offered.

Illinois State University—see Textile Programs

Incarnate Word College, San Antonio, Texas 78209
Urban environment; coed; Roman Catholic college started in 1900; dormitory facilities; 100 scholarships, grants, student loans, work-study programs available.

Indiana State University, Terre Haute, Indiana 47809
Urban environment, concentrated campus; coed; residence halls with dining facilities; 2,000 scholarships, loans, part-time employment, work-study available; at least half of the students earn all or part of their expenses.

Indiana University of Pennsylvania, Indiana, Pennsylvania 15701
Small-city environment, northeast of Pittsburgh; coed; state-owned and controlled; dormitory and residence facilities; limited academic scholarships available for incoming first-year students; loans, work-study programs offered; one-third of the students earn part of their expenses.

Iowa Lakes Community College, Estherville, Iowa 51334
Formerly known as Emmetsburg Jr. College; regional accreditation.

Jefferson Community College, P.O. Box 473, Watertown, New York 13601
Coed; publicly controlled; first-year students admitted with a high school diploma or the equivalent; no dormitory facilities; A.A., A.S., A.A.S., A.O.S. degrees and certificates awarded.

Jones College, 1505 E. Colonial Drive, Orlando, Florida 32803
Private senior college; accepts students in September, December, March, June; B.S., A.B., B.B.A. degrees awarded.

Kansas State University, Manhattan, Kansas 66502
Small-city environment; coed; founded in 1863; admits any graduate of accredited Kansas high school and out-of-state students who show promise of academic success; dormitory facilities; scholarships, student loans, athletic grants-in-aid programs available; intercollegiate athletics offered.

Kensington University, 512 E. Wilson Avenue, Glendale, California 91209

Urban, greater Los Angeles area; institution founded in 1976; students must qualify for the last year of the degree program by submitting transcripts and resume of life-learning experiences; off-campus program; students placed on Independent Study Plan.

Kent State University, Kent, Ohio 44242

Small-city environment, near Akron and Cleveland; coed; founded in 1910; new students admitted September, January, March, June; all graduates of Ohio high schools eligible for admission, but graduates of other states must meet out-of-state requirements; residence hall facilities; scholarships and loans available; intercollegiate athletics offered.

Kirkwood Community College, 6301 Bowling Street S. W., Cedar Rapids, Iowa 52406

Coed; public college; approved housing facilities; associate degree awarded.

Laboratory Institute of Merchandising, 12 East 33rd Street, New York, New York 10022

Urban environment; coed; privately supported school founded in 1939; scholarships, grants-in-aid offered.

Lincoln College, Lincoln, Illinois 62656

Coed; privately endowed; 500 students; dormitory facilities; A.A. degree and certificates awarded.

Los Angeles Harbor College, Wilmington, California 90744

Coed; operated by the Los Angeles Community College District; open admissions to graduates of accredited high schools or to adults 18 years or older giving evidence of the ability to profit from instruction; no dormitory facilities; no tuition; A.A. degree and Certificates awarded.

Los Angeles Trade-Technical College, 400 W. Washington Boulevard, Los Angeles, California 90015

Coed; adults 18 years or older or high school graduates may apply; operated by the Los Angeles Board of Education; no dormitory facilities, nearby housing available; no tuition for California residents; A.A., A.S. degrees awarded.

Lubbock Christian College, Lubbock, Texas 79407
Four-year liberal arts college founded in 1957; church-related; coed; dormitory facilities; intercollegiate athletics offered; scholarships available.

Mankato State University—see Textile Programs

Mansfield State College, Mansfield, Pennsylvania 16933
Small-town environment, state-controlled college; founded in 1857; dormitory facilities; loans, scholarships, work-study programs available; intercollegiate athletics offered.

Marist College, Poughkeepsie, New York 12601
Small-city environment; founded in 1929; first-year students enter September, January; coed; residence hall facilities; scholarships, loans, student employment available; B.A. degree awarded.

University of Maryland, College Park, Maryland 20742
Suburban environment; state university; founded in 1856; coed; dormitory facilities; scholarships, grants, loans available; more than half of the students earn all or part of their expenses.

Marymount College, Tarrytown, New York 10591
Twenty miles north of New York City; campus overlooks the Hudson River; women's college founded by the Religious Order of the Sacred Heart of Mary in 1918; first-year students admitted September, January; scholarships, loans, and campus employment available; B.A., B.S. degrees awarded.

Marymount College of Virginia, Arlington, Virginia 22207
Suburban environment 20 minutes from Washington, D.C.; women's Roman Catholic college; A.A., A.A.S., B.A. degrees awarded.

Marywood College, Scranton, Pennsylvania 18509
Suburban, residential environment; liberal arts college for women; founded in 1915; scholarships awarded on the basis of need; loans available.

University of Massachusetts, Amherst, Massachusetts 01002
Small-town, rural environment; coed; state-controlled school founded in 1863; admissions September, January; residence hall facilities; scholarships, ample loan funds, and college employment opportunities available; one-third of the students earn all or part of their expenses.

Massachusetts College of Art, Boston, Massachusetts 02215
Urban environment; coed; state-controlled institution; art portfolio required; no dormitory facilities, B.F.A. degree awarded.

Miami-Jacobs Jr. College of Business, 400 E. Second Street,
Dayton, Ohio 45402
Downtown location; private; coed; housing and eating facilities nearby; A.B. degree programs, related part-time employment for the students.

Michigan State University—see Textile Programs

Middle Tennessee State University, Murfreesboro, Tennessee 37132
Small-city environment; coed; founded in 1911; students admitted September, January, June; dormitory facilities; scholarships and loans available.

Midland College, 3600 N. Garfield, Midland, Texas 79701
Coed; first-year students admitted upon high school graduation, with equivalency diploma or individual approval; no housing facilities; intercollegiate athletics offered; associate degrees and certificates awarded.

University of Minnesota—see Textile Programs

University of Mississippi, University, Mississippi 38677
In northern Mississippi; coed; state-controlled school; founded in 1848; dormitory facilities; scholarships available (some for Mississippi residents only); intercollegiate sports offered.

Moorhead State University—see Textile Programs

Mt. Aloysius Jr. College, Cresson, Pennsylvania 16630
Coed; private; 2-year Catholic institution.

Mt. Mary College, Milwaukee, Wisconsin 53222
Suburban environment; women's Roman Catholic college run by School Sisters of Notre Dame; founded in 1872; dormitory facilities; scholarships, grants-in-aid available; B.S. degree awarded.

Mount San Antonio College, Walnut, California 91789
Coed; intercollegiate sports offered, no dormitory facilities; no tuition for California residents; no fees; free transportation provided; A.A. degree awarded.

Mt. Vernon College, 2100 Foxhall Road, N W, Washington D. C. 20007
Two-year and 4-year private women's college; A.A., B.A. degrees awarded

University of Nebraska—see Textile Programs

University of New Haven, West Haven, Connecticut 06516
Private; coed; founded in 1920; first-year students admitted September, January; limited dormitory facilities; loans, grants, scholarships; work-study programs available; intercollegiate sports offered.

University of North Alabama, Florence, Alabama 35630
Urban environment; coed; state-supported school; founded in 1855; dormitory facilities; limited scholarships, loan funds.

University of North Carolina, Greensboro, North Carolina 27412
Urban environment; coed; state-supported; dormitory facilities; limited scholarships, loan funds available.

North Carolina State University—see Textile Programs

North Dakota State University, Fargo, North Dakota 58102
Urban; coed; state-controlled; dormitory facilities; 300 scholarships averaging $300 each; loan fund; many students earn all or part of expenses.

Northeast Mississippi Jr. College, Booneville, Mississippi 38829
Coed; dormitory facilities; A.A. degree awarded.

Northern Michigan University—see Textile Programs

Oakton Community College, Des Plaines, Illinois 60016
Coed; founded in 1969; A.A., A.A.S. degrees.

Ohio State University—see Textile Programs

Ohio University, Athens, Ohio 45701
Small-city; coed; state-assisted institution; founded in 1804; the first institution of higher learning in the Northwest Territory; dormitory and residence hall facilities; 250 entering first-year students scholarships available; intercollegiate sports offered; university owns and operates airport.

University of Oklahoma, Norman, Oklahoma 73019
Urban environment; coed; state-controlled school; founded in 1890; students admitted August, January, June; dormitory facilities; $200,000 scholarship fund, loans, and work-study programs available.

Pace University, Pace College Plaza, New York 10038
Urban, downtown environment; coed; private school; founded in 1906; students admitted September, February; intercollegiate sports; grants, loans, scholarships awarded on need and academic achievement.

Parsons School of Design, 66 Fifth Avenue, New York 10011
Urban environment; coed; private institution that is a division of the New School for Social Research; students admitted September, January; introductory summer session available for high school students; exchange programs with other art colleges.

Philadelphia College of Textiles and Science—see Textile Programs

Purdue University, West Lafayette, Indiana 47907
Small-city environment near Indianapolis; coed; state-controlled land-grant college; founded in 1869; residence hall facilities; scholarships and loans available.

Radford College—see Textile Programs

Riverside City College, Riverside, California 92506
Coed; open admissions; no dormitory or dining facilities; A.A. degree awarded.

Rochester Institute of Technology—see Textile Programs

Rosary College—see Textile Programs

San Joaquin Delta, Stockton, California 95204
Coed; 2-year public junior college; A.A. degree awarded.

Schreiner College, Kerrville, Texas 78028
Coed; junior college related to the Presbyterian Church; first-year students admitted on diploma in August, January, June; dormitory facilities; A.A. degree awarded.

Seattle Pacific University—see Textile Programs

Seminole Community College, Sanford, Florida 32771
Coed; publicly controlled institution; A.A., A.S. degrees awarded.

Skyline College, San Bruno, California 94066
Coed; tuition free for California residents; A.A. degree awarded; first-year students admitted on high school diploma or equivalent; persons 18 years or older admitted on evidence of the ability to profit from instruction; no dormitory facilities.

Southeast Missouri State College, Cape Girardeau, Missouri 63701
Small-city environment on the Mississippi River; coed; state institution; residence halls available; some scholarships and loan funds for qualified students.

College of St. Benedict, St. Joseph, Minnesota 56374
Seventy miles northwest of Minneapolis; women's private college founded in 1913 by Sisters of Saint Benedict; dormitory facilities; scholarships, grants-in-aid, work-study programs; campus employment available.

College of St. Theresa, Winona, Minnesota 55987
City environment in Mississippi Valley; private women's college founded in 1907 by the Sisters of St. Francis; residential facilities for women; classes open to male and female commuters; scholarships and financial aid available.

St. Vincent's College—see Textile Programs

Steed College, Johnson City, Tennessee 37601
Coed; nonprofit institution; founded in 1940; nonsectarian; first-year students enter any quarter and are admitted on certificate and high school referral; 20 scholarships and financial aid available.

Stephens College, Columbia, Missouri 65215
Small-city environment; nondenominational, residential women's college; residence hall facilities; scholarships, grants-in-aid, campus employment, loan programs available.

Syracuse University—see Textile Programs

Tarleton State College, Stephenville, Texas 76402
Part of Texas A & M University system; coed.

University of Tennessee—see Textile Programs

Texas Christian University, Fort Worth, Texas 76129
Urban setting; coed; privately controlled institution related to Christian Church (Disciples of Christ); founded in 1873; dormitory facilities; opportunities for scholarships, financial aid, and employment.

Texas Southern University, Houston, Texas 77004
Urban setting; coed; state-supported institution; founded in 1947; limited scholarships available.

Texas Tech University, Lubbock, Texas 79409
Small-city environment; coed; state-supported institution founded in 1925; dormitory facilities; about 225 scholarships available, most based on outstanding achievement rather than on need; loan fund.

Texas Woman's University, Denton, Texas 76204
Urban environment 30 miles north of Dallas-Fort Worth metropolitan area; women's state-supported university founded in 1903; 100 students, free tuition to Texas high school female valedictorians.

Thornton Community College, South Holland, Illinois 60473
Coed; open door admissions policy to persons 18 years of age or older; no dormitory facilities; A.A. degree and certificates awarded.

Utah State University—see Textile Programs

Ventura College—see Textile Programs

Vincennes University, 1002 N. First Street, Vincennes, Indiana 47591
Coed; tax-supported junior college by Knox County and the state of Indiana; students admitted on evidence of high school ratings; dormitory facilities; associate degrees awarded.

Virginia Commonwealth University—see Textile Programs

Virginia Polytechnic Institute and State University, Blacksburg, Virginia 24061
Small-city environment, 40 miles west of Roanoke; state-controlled land-grant university established in 1872; coed; scholarships, loans, financial aid available.

Washington International College, 814 20th Street, NW, Washington, D.C. 20006
　　Opened in 1971; A.A. and B. A. degrees awarded.

Washington State University, Pullman, Washington 99163
　　Small-town environment 80 miles south of Spokane; coed; state-controlled land-grant school; founded in 1890; dormitory facilities; over 500 scholarships, loans, part-time job opportunities, including work-study program, which offers summer jobs throughout the state.

Washington University, St. Louis, Missouri 63130
　　Urban-suburban setting; coed; non-sectarian; privately controlled school established in 1853; residence hall facilities.

Wayne State College, Wayne, Nebraska 68787
　　Small-city environment; state-controlled; coed; dormitory facilities; scholarship and loans available.

Wayne State University—see Textile Programs

West Valley College, 14000 Fruitvale Avenue, Saratoga, California 95070
　　A.A. and A.S. degrees awarded.

University of Wisconsin—see Textile Programs

VGM C...

VGM Career Horizons
a division of NTC *Publishing Group*
4255 West Touhy Avenue
Lincolnwood, Illinois 60646-1975